ESCOFFIER'S
COOK BOOK OF
DESSERTS, SWEETS, AND ICES

MOULDS

Easter Egg

Porcelain Cases

Pound Cake

Cassolet

Gratin

Dome

Ice Cream

Cutlet

Bombe

Terrine à Paté

Tartlet —
Croustade

Ornamental Border

Brioche

Madeleine

Parfait

Charlotte

Salamander

Conical —
Pyramid

Cocotte

Dariole — Baba
Timbale

Petit Four

Star

Larding Needle

Spring-Form —
Flawn-Ring

Tart

Savarin —
Ring — Border

ESCOFFIER'S
COOK BOOK OF
DESSERTS, SWEETS,
AND ICES

by A. ESCOFFIER

CRESCENT BOOKS, INC.

New York

WEIGHTS AND MEASUREMENTS

1 quart	=	4 cups	=		64 tbsp.
1 pint	=	2 cups	=		32 tbsp.
$\frac{1}{2}$ pint	=	1 cup	=		16 tbsp.
$\frac{1}{3}$ pint	=	$\frac{2}{3}$ cup	=		$10\frac{2}{3}$ tbsp.
$\frac{1}{4}$ pint	=	$\frac{1}{2}$ cup	=		8 tbsp.
$\frac{1}{6}$ pint	=	$\frac{2}{6}$ cup	=	app.	$6\frac{1}{2}$ tbsp.
1 tbsp.	=				3 tsp.

BUTTER, One pound	=	2 cups
FLOUR, One pound	=	4 cups
SUGAR, One pound	=	$2\frac{1}{4}$ cups
1 tbsp. CORNSTARCH	=	$\frac{1}{2}$ ounce
1 tbsp. FLOUR	=	$\frac{1}{4}$ ounce

This edition published by Crescent Books, Inc.,
a division of Crown Publishers, Inc.

(A)

PUBLISHERS' NOTE

ESCOFFIER'S COOK BOOK OF DESSERTS, SWEETS, AND ICES is taken from THE ESCOFFIER COOK BOOK, the American translation of the great French Master Chef's world-famous *Guide Culinaire*. Although everything in it has been stated in American terms and in accordance with American usage, the publishers have nonetheless been careful to retain the precise sense of Escoffier's writing. Therefore, Escoffier's recipes for certain foreign foods not usually obtainable in the United States have been retained for the benefit of those who may desire them. In such cases, the recipes state the American equivalents of the foreign foods.

Likewise, French cooking terms (for instance, *poëling,* which means roasting with butter) have been used throughout the book because they often do not bear exact translation. However, these terms are fully explained in context in the recipes where they appear as well as in the Glossary. Terms defined in the Glossary are printed in italics in the recipes.

When, in one recipe, M. Escoffier refers to another recipe, that recipe number is given in parentheses. The numbers used with each recipe are from the original Escoffier numbering system. Numbers out of sequence can be found in the Appendix in the back of the book.

The discussions preceding each type of food are eminently interesting and informative. The publishers suggest that readers consult these before proceeding with the preparation of any of the excellent dishes described.

CONTENTS

GLOSSARY

Abats, refers to such butcher's specialties as heads, hearts, liver, kidneys, giblets, etc.

Aiguilettes, these are simply the breasts of the fowl cut into very thin slices.

Ailerons (wings).

Amourettes, the spinal marrow of the calf.

Anglaise, to treat à la Anglaise, see No. 174. Or to cook à la Anglaise, means to cook plainly in water. Also a preparation of beaten eggs and seasoning and oil.

Aromatics, No. 174a, this term mainly pertains to seasonings and herbs, but in many cases the author has used it to indicate a vegetable garnish, such as carrots, onions, etc., as in the preparation of a *Poëlé,* see No. 250.

Attereaux, bits of meat cooked on small skewers.

Baba mould, see Drawing.

Bain-marie, a hot water bath used for cooking or for keeping warm various preparations. At times an ordinary double-boiler will serve the same purpose, if the recipe indicates small quantities.

Barquettes, these are simply boat-shaped pastry shells used for garnishing.

Bavarois, this is the Bavarian Cream.

Biscottes, these are a light kind of dry rusk.

Bisque, see No. 241.

Blanched, see No. 273.

Bombe mould, see Drawing.

Border mould, see Drawing.

Braising, see Nos. 247 and 248. The traditional French method of braising is apt to be confusing so it is best to consult the chapters on this subject, which explain in detail. For other types of braisings consult the index.

Brandade, see No. 127, a mixture of a sauce and shredded fish, usually salt cod.

Brioche mould, see Drawing.

Brochettes, means to stick small pieces of meat on a skewer and cook in this manner.

Brunoise fashion, to cut food into small dice.

Caramel Sugar or Stage, see No. 2344.

Casserole (En), see No. 250.

Cassolet Mould, see Drawing.

Cèpes, a kind of mushroom.

Charlotte Mould, see Drawing.

Chartreuse, see No. 1220.

Chiffonade, see No. 215.

Choux, a kind of cake made from pâte a Choux. (Cream Puff Paste).

Civet, this is jugged hare.

Cocotte Mould, see Drawing.

Court-Boullion, see page 64.

Croustade Mould, see Drawing.

Croutons, pieces of bread in various shapes and sizes, fried in butter. Aspic jelly croutons are used to garnish cold dishes or salads.

vii

Cullis, see No. 240.

Cutlet Mould, see Drawing.

Dariole Mould, see Drawing.

Darne, see No. 270, this is simply a large slice or cut, usually of salmon or other large fish.

Dome Mould, see Drawing.

Duxelles, see page 94.

Egg Mould, see Drawing.

Émincé, this simply means that the food is cut into a fine mince.

Essence, see Nos. 13 and 2354. The word essence when applied to meats, vegetables, etc., means a concentrate of that particular product, but when indicated in a pastry or dessert recipe it means flavoring or extract.

Fecula, this is pure starch and is principally used for thickening. Cornstarch, flour, etc., may be used.

Feuilletés, these are little pastries made of puff pastry in oval, round, or other shapes, used for appetizers, soups, etc.

Fines Herbes, see No. 174a. Minced fine dry herbs. But if the recipe calls for a herb sauce, see No. 132.

Flawn-ring (Spring-form), see Drawing.

Flute, a long crisp French dinner roll used in soups.

Foie-Gras, fat goose liver which is sometimes used uncooked or cooked in the recipes. At other times it is the prepared pâté type which is called for.

Fondue, it is either a cheese preparation or a pulpy state to which vegetables like tomatoes, sorrel, etc., are reduced by cooking.

Forcemeat, see page 78 under stuffings and forcemeat.

Fricandeau, is a large larded slice of veal from off the rump, similar to the Wiener Schnitzel.

Fumet, see No. 11. This is a kind of concentrated essence extracted from fish, game, by slow cooking.

Galette, any food formed into the shape of a small cake or patty.

Garbures, this is nothing more than a thick vegetable soup or hodge-podge.

Gaufrette, a thin wafer used in dessert preparations and for garnishes.

Glaze, the author has used this term to indicate a method of procedure in the use of concentrated essence which gives a glossy covering, and it may differ according to the recipe in which it is used. Therefore it is important that the reader refer to the index, according to whether the recipe calls for meat, game, fish, etc.

Godiveau, see No. 198

Granité, is very much like a sherbet.

Gratin or Gratined, see Nos. 268 to 272 inclusive.

Gratin Dish or Mould, see Drawing.

Grenadin, are small slices of veal on the order of very small veal cutlets, prepared according to the given recipe.

Ice Cream Mould, see Drawing.

Jardinières, this is a vegetable soup or sauce, or a mode of garnishing with garden vegetables.

Julienne, means to cut a product into long matched-shaped sticks.

Lard, See Stud (Glossary).

Larding Needle, see Drawing.

Lenten, simply means cooking without meat.

Macédoine, this is a mixture of early season vegetables and/or fruit.

Madeleine Mould, see Drawing.

Maigre (lean), refers to any dish prepared in the Lenten style, meaning without meat.

Maintenon, see No. 226.

Manié (butter and flour), see No. 151.

Manque Mould, a fancy mould.

Marinade or Marinate, see pages 64 to 69, inclusive. Means the liquid and to soak or steep the product in a prepared sauce or liquid prior to cooking it.

Matelotes, see Nos. 1037–38.

Matignon, see No. 227.

Mignonette, this is a peeled finest quality peppercorn.

Milt, this is another name for fish roe.

Minion Fillets, when used in a recipe for poultry or fowl of any kind, game birds, etc., it pertains to that part of the breast meat that lies right next to the *Suprême,* the largest muscles in the poultry breast. In the four footed animals it is the tenderloin.

Mirepoix, see No. 228.

Mise-en-Place, a general name given to those elementary preparations which are constantly resorted to during the various stages of most culinary operations.

Mousses, a class of light, hot or cold preparations of fish, meat, poultry, etc., and sweets, formed in large moulds large enough to serve a number of persons.

Mousselines, this is the same preparation as the *Mousse,* except that it is made in individual moulds.

Noisettes, these are small kernels of meat like the center part of a rib chop. It is really a part of the tenderloin like the tournedos of beef.

Oxalis Roots, this is a Mexican vegetable with a leaf similar to sorrel. It is a tuberous plant and the roots are very much like the ordinary potato and the latter or the Jerusalem artichoke may be used to replace it.

Orgeat, this is a preparation from orange-flower water, sugar and almonds, made into a thick syrup.

Ornamented Border Mould, see Drawing.

Palmettes, palm-shaped pieces of puff paste used in decorating.

Panada, see No. 189 under stuffings and forcemeat.

Panés à la Anglaise, see No. 174. Means covered with bread-crumbs.

Pannequets, similar to pancakes.

Papillote means wrapping the preparation in vegetable parchment and cooking it that way in the oven.

Parfait Mould, see Drawing.

Pâte à Choux is the kind of paste used for ordinary cream puff shells.

Pauppiette, any preparation rolled into a roulade or scroll and cooked in a like manner.

Paysanne, to cut the food or product into triangles.

Petit Four Mould, see Drawing.

Pig's Caul, this is the investing membrane, with fatty veins, which covers the intestinal organs of the pig. It is used by butchers in the preparation of certain cuts of meat for cooking and is therefore difficult to procure except at slaughter houses.

Pluches, principally applied to Chervil, but they may be the serrated portions of any leaves, such as tarragon, mint, etc.

Poach, see No. 249. This term means cooking very slowly in small amounts of water at the lowest temperature. It is best to refer to the description when in doubt about the method used.

Poëlé, see No. 250. A method of cooking used in France which should be called simply "butter roasting." It applies not only to meats, but to eggs, etc.

Porcelain Cases, see Drawing.

Pound Cake Mould, see Drawing.

Printanier, this usually means a garnish or filling of early spring vegetables cut into various shapes. It may also apply to preparations comprising the same.

Profiterolles, see No. 218.

Provençale, see No. 235. This is a special blend of Bechamel, with eggs and seasoning, used for stuffing foods, particularly cutlets a la Provençale.

Purée, a purée is any food that is strained through a sieve, so that it forms a complete mass. The consistency of the product referred to in the recipe and its use governs this. Purée not only applies to soups or sauces, etc., but to fruits, vegetables, meats, etc. In other words, any food.

Pyramid Mould, see Drawing.

Quenelle, see No. 205. These are forcemeat balls used for garnishing soup, etc.

Râble, the back or saddle of a hare.

Raspings, see No. 178. Simply the grated crusts of bread, etc., used for gratins, a l'Anglaise, etc.

Ravioli, an Italian form of filled paste, which is boiled and covered with a sauce.

Richelieu Mould, a deep fluted mould.

Risotta or Rizotto, is an Italian national dish. Rice, cooked with saffron and olive oil.

Rissole, this term when pertaining to meats means to sear or brown with a protective crust. In regard to cakes, fritters, etc., it means to coat them with a golden brown crust.

Roulade, this is the more general name for *Pauppiette.*

Royales, see No. 213.

Salamander, this is a large sheet of iron on which are heaped red hot coals, so that if one holds this against a dish it browns or glazes it, almost at once. A clean coal shovel may be used for the same purpose. See Drawing.

Salpicon, a compound of various products, cut into dice and generally combined with a sauce or a forcemeat.

Sauté, see No. 251.

Savarin Mould, see Drawing.

Soufflé, a name given to a class of light, hot or cold preparations of fish, meat, poultry, etc. Also to sweets to which the whites of eggs are added if the preparation is served hot, and to which whipped cream is added if it is served cold.

Spring-Form, see Drawing.

Star Mould, see Drawing.

Swashing or Swirling, when referred to, it actually means scraping from the utensil used the adhered particles and diluting it with the wine or liquid indicated in the recipe.

Stud or Lard, studding is done by injecting protruding pieces of fat into the incisions made in the meat with a sharp knife. Larding uses the same strip of fat or bacon, which are inserted into a larding needle. With this, one pinches the meat at regular intervals allowing the larding fat to show at the point of its entry. See Drawing.

Subrics are really spinach puffs.

Supreme, this is the name given to the fillet or the breast of fowl. The term has

Tart Mould, see Drawing.

Tartlet Mould, see Drawing.

Tazza Mould, Fancy cup mould.

Terrine, this is a patty and its container. But a terrine à pâté is an earthenware dish in which a patty or food is cooked. See Drawing.

Timbale, may mean a *Timbale* Mould and it may mean a food cooked in the Mould or crust, and formed in such a manner. See Drawing.

Verjuice, this is the juice of unripe fruit, such as grapes, etc. Sometimes used as a substitute for vinegar in acidulating water.

Vesiga is the dried spine-marrow of the sturgeon and very difficult to procure.

Zest, the outermost, colored glossy film of the rind of an orange or lemon.

CHAPTER I

PASTRY, Confectionery, and Ices are so closely allied to Cookery, and they are so surely its complements, that it is impossible to omit them when dealing with Entremets, even though the latter be limited to the kind proper to the kitchen.

However, these subjects, which could supply matter for voluminous works, are too complex for it to be possible to cope thoroughly with them here.

I shall therefore confine myself to the expounding of their fundamental principles and the essential operations relating thereto, a knowledge of which is absolutely necessary for the successful preparation of Kitchen Entremets and Ices. The directions given hereafter are certainly too inadequate to convert an ordinary cook into a pastry-cook, a confectioner, or an icing cook ("glacier"); but they will at least permit of his carrying out a complete dinner, if the necessity so to do should occur.

ELEMENTARY PREPARATIONS OF PASTRY WHICH MAY BE APPLIED TO ENTREMETS

2338—VARIOUS ALMOND PREPARATIONS

Préparations Diverses d'amandes

It is important that one should have shelled, skinned, slivered, and chopped almonds.

To Skin Almonds.—Throw them in a saucepan of boiling water, place the utensil on the side of the fire without allowing the boiling to continue, and let the almonds soak for seven or eight minutes. As soon as the skin slips when pressing them between one's fingers, turn them out into a strainer; cool them in cold water, and skin them. This done, wash them in cold water; drain them well; spread them on a very clean pan, and dry them in a mild oven.

Slivered Almonds.—Having skinned and washed the almonds,

1

split them in two, and cut each half into five or six lengthwise slivers. Dry the latter in the warming-oven, and place them in the front of the oven for a while to color slightly.

They serve for nougat, and sometimes take the place of pine-nuts.

Chopped Almonds.—Having skinned the almonds, slightly dry them and chop them; rub them through a sieve, the coarseness of which should be in accordance with that required for the chopped almonds.

Spread the almonds on a pan covered with a sheet of paper, and dry them in the warming-oven, stirring them from time to time.

Toasted Almonds.—These are either slivered or chopped almonds set to bake on a pan in a moderate oven. Be sure to stir them frequently, that they may brown evenly, and take them out when they are of a nice golden shade.

Pralined Almonds.—Proceed as for toasted almonds, but sprinkle them frequently with icing sugar, which turns to caramel under the influence of the heat of the oven, and covers the almonds in a pale-brown coat of sugar.

2339—VARIOUS PREPARATIONS OF FILBERTS AND HAZEL-NUTS
Préparations Diverses de Noisettes

Filberts are a large kind of hazel-nut, generally covered with reddish skins.

After having cracked and removed the shells, put the filberts in a pan, and place them in the oven until their skins are slightly grilled. They need then only be rubbed between the fingers in order to clear them of their skins. Chopped filberts are prepared like chopped almonds, and should be included on the permanent handy shelf of the pastry cook.

2340—VARIOUS BUTTERS   *Beurres Divers*

Softened Butter.—More particularly in winter, when it is very hard, butter should be softened by being thoroughly kneaded in a towel to extract the butter-milk, which is always present in more or less large quantities; and to make the butter sufficiently soft to mix with the various ingredients of which the pastes are made.

Creamy Butter.—After having well softened it as above, put it in a bowl, previously rinsed with hot water and thoroughly wiped.

Work the butter with a spatula or a wooden spoon until it acquires the consistency of a cream—a necessary condition for certain of its uses.

Clarified Butter.—In pastry, clarified butter is used more especially for the buttering of moulds. Put the butter to be clarified into a saucepan, and cook it over a very slow fire until the casein substances liberated in the cooking process have accumulated and solidified on the bottom of the saucepan and the butter appears transparent, of a golden color, and gives off a slight, nutty odor.

Strain it through muslin, and put it aside until required.

2341—THE BUTTERING AND GLAZING OF MOULDS
Pour Beurrer et Glacer des Moules

All moulds, large and small, should be buttered to ensure the easy turning-out of cakes cooked in them. Clarified butter, owing to its purity, is the best for the purpose. It may be applied with a brush, care being taken that all the inside surfaces get uniformly covered. One unbuttered spot is sufficient to make a moulding stick, or to completely spoil a cake.

For certain cakes, chopped or slivered almonds are sprinkled in the mould. For others, especially biscuits, the moulds are flour-dusted—that is to say, a film of very dry flour or *fecula* (cornstarch, etc.) is allowed to settle on the layer of butter, which, at the turning out, appears like a *glazed* crust upon the cake.

2342—HOW TO BEAT THE WHITES OF EGGS
Façon de Fouetter les Blancs d'Oeufs

The best utensil for the purpose is a copper or stainless steel bowl in which the whisk or beater may act at all points owing to the spherical shape of the receptacle. Tinned or enamelled utensils set up a kind of greasiness which does not permit the whites to stiffen enough for some purposes.

Before beating the whites gently, and draw them up with the beater until all their molecules have disintegrated and they begin to thicken. They may then be beaten until they are sufficiently stiff to be taken up bodily by the whisk or beater.

Preventive Methods.—To facilitate the beating of whites of eggs, there may be added to them at the start a pinch either of salt or alum per ten whites. When, towards the close of the operation, the whites begin to separate, owing to any one of the various causes, add immediately one tablespoon of powdered sugar per ten whites, and then beat briskly, to restore them to their normal state.

2343— VEGETABLE COLORING MATTERS   *La coloration Végétale*

Every pastry-cook's stock should include a series of vegetable coloring matters, comprising carmine, liquid spinach green, yellow, etc.

When required, the blending of these colors yields the intermediate tones. The colors may be bought.

2344—THE COOKING OF SUGAR   *Le Cuisson du Sucre*

From the state of syrup to the most highly-concentrated state in which it is used in pastry, sugar passes through various stages of cooking, which are:—The small thread (215° F.) and the large thread (222° F.), the small ball (236° F.) and the large ball (248° F.), the small crack (285° F.) and the large crack (315° F.). When the last state is overreached, the sugar has become caramel (360° F.).

Put the necessary quantity of sugar in a small, copper or stainless steel pot; moisten with enough water to melt it, and boil. Carefully remove the scum which forms, and which might cause the sugar to granulate.

As soon as the sugar begins to move stiffly in boiling, it is a sign that the water has almost entirely evaporated, and that the real cooking of the sugar has begun.

From this moment, with moistened fingers or a little piece of moistened linen, take care to remove the crystallized sugar from the sides of the utensil, lest it make the remaining portion turn.

The cooking of the sugar then progresses very rapidly, and the states of its various stages, coming one upon the other in quick succession at intervals of a few minutes, may be ascertained as follows:—

It has reached the *small-thread stage,* when a drop of it held between the thumb and the first finger forms small resistless strings when the thumb and finger are drawn apart.

It has reached the *large-thread stage,* when, proceeding in the same way, the strings formed between the parted finger and thumb are more numerous and stronger.

From this moment care must be taken to use cold water in order to ascertain the state of the sugar.

When a few minutes have elapsed after the test for the large-thread state, dip the end of the first finger, first into cold water, then into the sugar, and plunge it again immediately into the bowl of cold water, which should be at hand. The sugar taken from the finger forms a kind of soft ball, and it is this state which is called the *small ball.*

When, upon repeating the procedure, the sugar removed from the finger rolls into a firmer ball, the *large-ball stage* is reached.

After the cooking has continued for a few seconds longer, the sugar lying on the finger peels off in the form of a thin, flexible film, which sticks to the teeth. This is the *small-crack stage*. Tests should then be made in quick succession, until the film taken from the end of the finger breaks "clean" in the teeth, like glass. This is the *large-crack state,* the last of the cooking stages, and as soon as it has been reached the utensil should be taken off the fire, lest a few seconds more turn the sugar to *caramel.*

To prevent the granulating of the sugar, a few drops of lemon juice may be added to it; or, better still, a tablespoon of glucose per lb.

2345—OLD-FASHIONED GLAZE   *Glace à l'Ancienne*

Put the required amount of *icing sugar* (2346a) in a small saucepan, the quantity used being in proportion to the object to be glazed.

If it be flavored with vanilla, orange, or lemon, dilute it with a little water, keeping it somewhat stiff; add some vanilla-flavored sugar or grated orange-rind, and stir it up well for a few minutes. Then make it lukewarm, so that it may run easily and dry quickly, and pour it over the object to be treated.

For the above-mentioned flavors, an infusion of vanilla or orange-rind may be prepared, and this may serve in diluting the *glaze*. The flavors may also be used in the form of *essences,* provided it be remembered that they are usually very strong, and must be used with caution.

If liqueur *glazes* are in question, such as Kirsch, Rum, Anisette, Maraschino, etc., the *glaze* is diluted with the liqueur and made lukewarm as directed above.

2346—FONDANT GLAZE   *Glace au Fondant*

Preparation of the "Fondant."—Put some granulated sugar into a small saucepan, the quantity being in accordance with the amount of "Fondant" required.

Moisten with just enough water to melt the sugar, and set to cook as directed under "The Cooking of Sugar" (2344).

Stop the cooking precisely at 230° F. between the *large-thread stage* and the *small-ball stage,* and pour the sugar on a moderately-oiled marble slab. Let it half cool for a few minutes; then, with a spatula, move it about well in all directions, taking care that no portion of the sugar on the marble is left untouched by the spatula, for any such portion would harden and form lumps in the Fondant.

After ten to fifteen minutes' work with the spatula, the sugar should have become a white, slightly granulated paste. Heap the latter together, and scrape the marble slab with the blade of a strong knife. Carefully knead this paste (2357) with the palm of the hand until it is very thin and smooth, whereupon the Fondant is ready for use.

It need now only be heaped in a bowl, covered with a damp cloth, and kept somewhat dry.

To Glaze with "Fondant."—Put the required amount of it into a saucepan; work it over a slow fire for a while, in order to soften it, and moisten it, little by little, with water when a dry flavor or an *essence* is used, or, otherwise, with the selected liqueur.

Warm slightly in order to make the *glaze* very liquid and to ensure its speedy drying, and pour it, in one motion, over the object to be *glazed*.

With the help of some color, the *glaze* is generally given the tint of the fruit which flavors it.

2346a—ICING SUGAR   *Sucre en Glace*

(In the United States there is available every quality of finest confectioners' sugar for icing. In Europe the following method was used.—Ed.)

The sugar is strained through a taut and fine silk sieve. The sugar strained through this silk has the delicacy of starch. At times it is used instead of Fondant for the *glazing* of cakes, but it is mostly used for white and caramel *glazings*. For this purpose the sugar is held in a tin box, covered with a lid pierced with small holes, called a sugar dredger.

To glaze (or sprinkle) white is to cover a cake, a fritter, or another object with a coat of icing sugar. This operation is done by shaking the sugar dredger over the object to be sprinkled.

To glaze with caramel is to cover a *Soufflé*, a *souffléd* omelet, fruit fritters, a custard, or other objects with a coat of icing sugar, by placing the sugar-coated object in intense heat a few minutes, to melt the sugar, which is converted into a brilliant, glossy covering of caramel.

2347—SUGAR GRAINS   *Les Paillettes de Sucre*

These are used in pastry to border certain cakes, or to surround the sugared-paste bases on which cakes are set. For this purpose the parts to which the sugar is expected to adhere must be spread with cooked apricot syrup.

To make them, take some sugar and sift it, first through a coarse strainer and then through a finer one, according to the size the sugar grains are required to be. The powder will, of course, fall and leave the grains clean.

2348—COLORED SUGAR GRAINS   *Sucre Coloré*

To color sugar grains, spread them on a piece of paper, and add a drop of liquid vegetable-coloring or a very little colored paste per tablespoon of sugar. The amount of coloring matter may either be lessened or increased, according to the shade required.

Rub the sugar in the hand to color it evenly; dry in a moderately warm drying-pan, and keep in a dry place in well-closed boxes.

(Colored sugar ready prepared is available in good grocery stores. —Ed.)

2349—VANILLA SUGAR   *Sucre Vanille*

The vanilla beans which have served in preparing infusions still possess some flavor. Reserve them, therefore, for the making of vanilla sugar.

After having gently dried them out, pound them finely with twice their weight of lump sugar; sift through the finest sieve, and again pound the bits remaining in the sieve until every particle goes through. Keep the preparation in a well-closed jar in a dry place.

(It is easier to make a good vanilla sugar nowadays by pounding the vanilla bean with finely powdered sugar, a little, and then allowing the mixture to remain in a tightly closed glass jar until the sugar is needed. You can replace the vanilla flavored sugar by fresh sugar and repeat the process. The bean will gradually lose its strength, but it will last for quite a while.—Ed.)

2350—CANDIED FRUIT   *Fruits Crystalisés*

These are used in the decoration of certain cakes, and as the in-gredients of others.

They comprise angelica, golden and green preserved kumquats, cherries, plums, red and white pears, etc.

Candied fruit may be bought ready-prepared.

2351—APPLE JELLY FOR DECORATING
Gelée aux Pommes pour Garnitures

Quarter, peel, and core the apples (preferably russets or tart apples), and throw them, one by one, in a bowl of fresh water to prevent their getting brown.

Then put them in a copper or stainless steel pot with one and one-half pints of water per two lbs. of apples, and cook them gently without touching them.

This done, pour off their juice, and return it to the pot together with two lbs. of sugar per quart. Boil; skim with great care, that the jelly may be clear, and cook over a hot fire until the jelly has reached a stage when, on taking the skimmer out of the pot, the jelly adhering to it seems to mass itself towards the middle of the skimmer; or when the jelly breaks up into large drops, separated one from the other.

Then take the jelly off the fire; add some carmine to it, drop by drop, until it acquires a rosy hue; strain it again through a fine piece of linen, that it may be transparent, and finally pour it into tin pans to cool.

Put aside until wanted.

2352—PRALIN
Pralin

If it be for the purpose of covering certain cakes, or for forming a *glaze* on a fruit *entremet,* prepare it thus:—Put the whites of two eggs and three tablespoons of icing sugar in a small pan. Mix and stir briskly with a small, wooden spoon, until the paste becomes somewhat thick. Then, subject to the purpose for which it is intended, add a more or less large quantity of chopped almonds, according to whether the *pralin* be required thick or slightly liquid for spreading. Cover it with a piece of white paper, moistened with white of egg, that it may remain moist if kept for some time.

If it is to be added to a *soufflé* preparation, to a *soufflé* omelet, to a preparation of ice, or to a custard, it is a nougat powder which is prepared as follows:—

Gently melt one lb. of powdered sugar in a small saucepan, taking care not to let it acquire a deeper shade than old gold. Mix twenty oz. of dried almonds with it; turn the whole out on to the corner of a slightly-oiled marble slab (or on an over-turned saucepan-lid), and leave to cool. When the nougat is quite cold, pound it and rub it through a sieve.

Pound and rub what remains in the sieve until the whole goes through.

Put the powder in a tightly closed jar, and place in a dry place.

2353—CURRANTS AND SULTANA RAISINS
Groseilles aux Grappes et Sultanas

Sultana raisins and currants should always be at hand, ready and cleaned. To clean them, first dredge them and then rub them in a towel, closed to form a sort of purse. Now, turn them into a sieve or colander, and shake vigorously, that the flour and the stems may be removed; then examine them, one by one, to make sure that no stems remain.

Currants should be examined with very particular care, as small stones often get in among them.

Put the currants and the sultana raisins aside, each in a canister or a jar.

2354—ESSENCES AND FLAVORINGS   *Essences et Assaissonements*

The various *essences* used in pastry are bought ready-made. The flavorings consist of those products treated by infusion, such as vanilla; of grated or infused products, such as lemon and orange peels; and liqueurs in general.

Fruit juices only become flavors when a liqueur in keeping with the fruit from which they were extracted has been added to them.

2355—GILDING PREPARATION   *La Préparation de la Dorure*

This consists of beaten eggs. Its purpose is to ensure the golden top coloring of certain cakes, to which it is applied with a brush. In some cases the eggs may be combined with a little water, as, for instance, when the heat of the oven is too hot, and cakes are required of a light color. In some cases, especially in that of small, dry cakes, it consists entirely of egg-yolks diluted with a few drops of water.

THE PASTES

2356—ORDINARY SHORT PASTE   *La Pâte Ordinaire*

Sift one lb. of flour over the mixing-board; make a hollow in the center, and put therein one-sixth oz. of salt, one-third pint of cold water, and one-half lb. of well softened butter. Mix the flour gradually with the butter and the water; mass the whole a moment or two, and knead it (2357) twice. Then roll it up in a ball; wrap it in a piece of linen that its surface may not dry, and put it aside in a cool place.

Remarks: A kneaded paste should be prepared either one day, or at least a few hours, in advance, in order that it may lose that elasticity which it acquires from the kneading.

Pastes, after they have rested awhile, are much more easily handled, and bake a much more definite and lighter brown, than those that are used as soon as they are prepared.

2357—THE KNEADING OF PASTES   *La Manipulation des Pâtes*

The object of kneading paste is to combine the ingredients of which it is composed thoroughly, and also to smooth it. Proceed as follows:—

When the paste is mixed, roll it into a mass; put it on the board; then press it away from you, little by little, between the board and the palm of the hand. For the paste to be perfectly smooth, it ought to be treated twice in this way.

2358—FINE, SHORT, OR FLAWN PASTE   *Pâte à Foncer Fine*

Sift one lb. of flour on the mixing-board, and hollow it in the center. Put in the hollow one-third oz. of salt, one and one-half oz. of powdered sugar, an egg, one-fourth pint of cold water, and ten oz. of butter. First, thoroughly mix the butter, the egg, the water, and the seasoning, and then gradually combine the flour with it.

Knead the paste; press it out twice; roll it into a ball; and wrap it up and set it aside in a cool place.

2359—PIE PASTE   *Pâte à Pâtés*

Take one lb. of sifted flour, four oz. of butter, one egg, one-third oz. of salt, and one-fourth pint of water. Mix as already directed; knead twice; roll up the paste, and set it in a cool place to rest. This paste should be kept somewhat firm.

2360—PIE PASTE WITH LARD   *Pâte pour Pâté au Lard*

Take one lb. of sifted flour, four oz. of lard, one-quarter pint of tepid water, one egg, one-third oz. of salt, and proceed exactly as in the case of (2359).

2361—DUMPLING AND PUDDING PASTES
Pâte à Dumplings et à Puddings

Break up ten oz. of very dry beef suet, and carefully clear it of all little pieces of skin and connective tissue. Chop it up as finely as possible; sift one lb. of flour on the mixing-board; hollow it out; and put into the hollow one-half oz. of salt, one and one-half oz. of sugar, one-third pint of water, and the chopped suet. Mix up these various ingredients, and, by degrees, combine the flour with them.

Mix the paste together, without kneading it, and put it aside in a cool place until it is wanted.

2362—DRY SUGARED PASTE FOR VARIOUS PURPOSES
Pâte Sèche Sucrée pour Différents Usages

Take one lb. of sifted flour, seven oz. of butter, five oz. of powdered sugar, three eggs, and one-half tablespoon of orange-flower water.

Mix in the usual way, knead it twice; roll it into a ball, and keep it wrapped up, in a cool place, until required.

2363—PASTE FOR SMALL TEA-CAKES   *Pâte à Petits Gateaux*

Take one lb. of sifted flour, ten oz. of butter, ten oz. of sugar, one egg, the yolks of four, and a tablespoon of orange-flower water.

Mix up gradually; mass the paste together, and roll it out into a thin layer, twice. Roll it up, and let it rest awhile in a cool place before it is used.

2364—GUMMING   *Gommer*

In the case of certain small cakes, especially those served at tea, it is possible to gum their surfaces in order to make them glossy. For this purpose a thin solution of gum arabic is used, and it is brushed over the cakes as they leave the oven, by means of a small brush.

Cakes may also be brushed with a syrup formed from milk and sugar, which mixture may be used instead of gum arabic with advantage.

2365—GALETTES PASTE   *Pâte à Galette Ordinaire*

Hollow out one lb. of sifted flour and put in its midst one-third oz. of salt, two oz. of powdered sugar, one-quarter pint of water, and one-half lb. of softened butter.

Mix, taking care to put in the flour only by degrees, knead thoroughly, that the ingredients may be well combined, and mass the paste together without making it too elastic. Leave it in a cool place for at least an hour; then roll it out three times, at intervals of eight minutes, for the reasons given under the directions for puff-paste.

2366—PUFF-PASTE   *Feuilletage*

Sift one lb. of flour on to the mixing-board. Make a hollow in it, and put in one-third oz. of table salt and about one-half pint of cold water, and mix without kneading. Mass the paste together, and let it rest for twenty minutes, that it may lose its elasticity, which will be all the more pronounced for its having been very much worked. It is to avoid this elasticity, therefore, that the mixing of puff-paste should be done with the smallest amount of kneading possible.

Spread the prepared paste on a flour-dusted board, in the shape of an even thin cake. Spread on one lb. of softened butter, without completely covering the paste; draw the edges of the paste towards the center, in such a way as to enclose the butter completely, and to form a square thickness of paste.

Leave to rest for ten minutes, and then begin the working of the paste; rolling it out to the length of one and one-half feet, and keeping it one in. thick. Fold this layer over three times, and press upon it with the rolling pin to join the superimposed layers. The whole of this operation constitutes one movement.

Begin another movement immediately, turning the paste the reverse way, and folding it as before. Set it to rest in a cool place for eight or ten minutes, and then do the same thing over twice more.

Ten minutes after the two last folding over actions (there should be six in all), the puff-paste is ready to be cut up and used.

Remarks relative to puff-paste: Good puff-paste should be buttered to the extent of one lb. per one and one-half lbs., that is, one lb. of butter for every one lb. of flour mixed with one-half pint of water. The consistency of the paste and the butter should be exactly the same, if they are to be evenly mixed; the butter ought therefore to be softened—more particularly in winter.

In preparing puff-paste, remember to put it in a cool place while it is resting; but never directly upon ice; for, though the ice would not affect the paste, it might seriously affect the butter.

It would harden it to the extent of preventing its perfect mixture with the mass, and lumps would form. Puff-paste should be rolled out very regularly, with the view of thoroughly distributing the butter throughout the preparation, and thus ensuring its uniform rising.

Puff-paste should not be worked too speedily; for, if it be so worked, it will be found to acquire an elasticity which not only makes it difficult to cut up, but also tends to make it shrink in the baking.

2367—PUFF-PASTE TRIMMINGS OR HALF PUFF-PASTE

Rognures ou Demi-Feuilletage

These are very useful in pastry work of the cook, for *tartlets, barquettes, croûtons,* etc. When the puff-paste is cut up, the trimmings should be rolled into a ball, and put aside in a cool place. Nevertheless they must be used within the space of two days in summer and four days in winter.

(They keep longer if protected by paper, in refrigerators.—Ed.)

2368—ORDINARY BRIOCHE PASTE   *Pate à Brioche Ordinaire*

Sift one lb. of flour on the board; take a quarter of it, make a hollow in it, and put in one-quarter oz. of very fresh, dry yeast. Mix the yeast and the flour with a little tepid water, so as to obtain a soft paste which is the leaven. Roll this paste into a ball; make two slits in its top, at right angles to one another, and place it in a small bowl.

Cover, and put it in a somewhat warm place, that the leaven may be sure to ferment.

Then make a hollow in the remaining flour, and put into it one-quarter oz. of salt, and one and one-half oz. of sugar, together with two tablespoons of milk to moisten it, one-third of the whole amount of the butter to be used, namely, four oz., and four eggs.

Begin by thoroughly mixing the butter, eggs and seasoning, and then combine the flour with it by degrees. When the paste forms a compact mass, knead and pull it about with the hands, that it may be light. When, at the end of a few minutes, it has acquired a certain resilience, make a hole in the middle of it and add one egg. Mix it with the paste; work it again, and after an interval of two minutes add one more egg in the same way. The total number of eggs for the quantities of other ingredients given above should be six.

Add the remaining butter (eight oz.) to the paste; the former being *manié* and even softened, just sufficiently to make it of the same consistency as the paste.

Spread it on, and mix the two; kneading small portions at a time. and combining those portions so as to mix the two elements completely.

At this stage, overturn the paste and spread the leaven (which should now be equal to twice its original bulk) upon it.

Mix it well as in the case of the butter, without working the paste.

Finally, put the paste into a bowl; cover it, and place it in a temperate place.

For it to have the desired lightness, this paste should rise for from ten to twelve hours. However, at the end of five or six hours, the process is arrested by the working of the paste; that is to say, by turning it out upon a flour-dusted board and beating it with the palm of the hand.

It is then returned to the bowl to rise again, for five or six hours; and then it is once more beaten just before being used.

(For the very dry yeast mentioned in all of the yeast recipes, the same amount of compressed yeast may be used, the only difference being that compressed yeast works much faster and more efficiently. Therefore the time for the rising of the fermented dough will be shortened.—Ed.)

2369—MOUSSELINE BRIOCHE PASTE   *Pâte à Brioche Mousseline*

Mousseline brioche paste is made from the ordinary kind (2368), combined with a little butter and developed in the mould by rising before the baking process—which procedure makes it exceedingly light and delicate.

This paste is used in the preparation of certain *timbales* for fruit desserts, and it is prepared as follows:—

Take the required amount of ordinary brioche paste, and add to it, per lb. of paste, two oz. of best butter, softened to the consistency of an ointment, that it may thoroughly mix with the paste. Roll the paste into a ball, and put it in a liberally-buttered mould, only filling it two-thirds. The remaining third of the mould is filled by the rising of the paste. Place the mould in a temperate place, until the paste has risen to the edges of the mould; brush the surface of the paste with melted butter, and bake in a moderate oven.

2370—ORDINARY BRIOCHE PASTE (FOR RISSOLES, SMALL PATTIES A LA DAUPHINE, AND VARIOUS OTHER PREPARATIONS)
Pâte à Brioche Commune

Quantities: One lb. of flour, seven oz. of butter, four fair-sized eggs, salt, a pinch of powdered sugar; one-third oz. of very dry, fresh yeast (see note in 2367), and a little tepid milk.

Make the leaven with a quarter of the flour, the yeast and the lukewarm milk, and set it to rise while the paste is being prepared.

Prepare the paste as already directed, and keep it rising as before for ten hours, taking care to arrest the process once.

The work is the same as in the preceding case, in every particular, except in regard to the amount of butter, which in this instance is only half as much; in regard to the amount of sugar, which should be just enough to ensure the coloring of the paste; and finally in regard to its firmness, which should permit the paste being worked with a rolling-pin.

2371—SAVARIN PASTE   *Pâte à Savarin*

Quantities: One lb. of flour; twelve oz. of butter; one-half oz. of very dry, fresh yeast; eight eggs; about one-third pint of milk; one-half oz. of salt, and one oz. of sugar.

Procedure: Savarin paste may be prepared in several ways; but the one given below is as simple and quick as could be desired.

Sift the flour into a round wooden bowl; hollow it out; add the yeast, and dissolve by means of tepid milk, stirring slightly with the tip of the finger.

Add the eggs; mix and work the paste by hand for a few minutes; scrape off those portions of it which have adhered to the side of the bowl, and add them to the whole.

Distribute the softened butter in small quantities over the paste. Cover, and set in a temperate place until the paste has risen to twice its original bulk. Then add salt; knead the paste, that it may thoroughly absorb the butter, and pat it briskly until it is sufficiently elastic to be taken up in one lump.

At this stage add the sugar, and work the paste again that the former may thoroughly mix with it. The sugar should only be added at the close of the operation; for, since it weakens the consistency of the paste, it would make it much more difficult to work were it added at the start.

THE USES OF THIS PASTE

If it be for Savarins with syrup, it is customary to sprinkle the previously-buttered moulds with slightly-grilled, chopped or slithered almonds. Take the paste in small quantities at a time, and line the moulds with it to the extent of one-third of their height.

The remaining two-thirds of each mould become covered when the paste rises owing to fermentation.

Proceed in the same way for Savarins which are to be kept dry.

for fruit crusts or other uses; but then the sprinkling of the moulds with almond may be omitted.

2372—BABA PASTE *Pâte à Baba*

Quantities: One lb. of flour; one-half lb. of butter; seven eggs; two-thirds oz. of yeast; one-fifth pint of milk; one-third oz. of salt; two-thirds oz. of sugar; three oz. of currants and sultana raisins in equal quantities.

Procedure: Proceed exactly as for Savarin paste, and add the currants and sultana raisins at the last with the sugar. In moulding, a few seeded Malaga raisins may be laid on the bottom of the moulds. As in the case of the Savarin, the paste should only fill one-third of the mould.

2373—ORDINARY CREAM PUFF PASTE *Pâte à Chou Ordinaire*

Quantities.—One pint of water; eight oz. of butter; one-third oz. of salt; one oz. of sugar; one lb. of sifted flour; sixteen fair-sized eggs, and a tablespoon of orange-flower water.

Procedure.—Put the water, butter, salt, and sugar in a saucepan and boil. When the liquid boils and rises, take the saucepan off the fire; add the flour, and mix. Return the saucepan to a moderate fire, and stir the paste until it ceases to stick to the spoon, and the butter begins to ooze slightly.

Take the saucepan off the fire; add the eggs, two at a time, taking care to mix them thoroughly with the paste before adding the succeeding ones. When all the eggs have been blended, finish the paste with orange-flower water.

2374—COMMON CREAM PUFF PASTE (FOR SOUFFLE FRITTERS, GNOCHI, POTATOES A LA DAUPHINE) *Pâte à Chou Commune*

Proceed as directed above, but reduce the quantity of butter to three oz., and the number of eggs to twelve; avoid drying this paste too much.

2375—RAMEKINS AND GOUGERE PASTE
Pâte à Ramequins et à Gougère

This is prepared exactly like ordinary "Pâte à Choux" (2373), except that:—

Milk takes the place of water.

The sugar and orange-flower water are omitted.

For the quantities given (2373), eight oz. of fresh Gruyère cheese,

cut into dice, are added to the paste, after all the eggs have been
beaten into it.

2376—FINE PASTE FOR SPONGE OR GENOISE

Pâte à Genoise Fine

Put into a bowl one lb. of powdered sugar and sixteen eggs. Mix
the two; place the basin upon hot coal cinders or on the side of the
fire, and beat its contents until they reach the *"ribbon" stage* (see
remarks below). Then add the selected flavoring (vanilla sugar,
orange rind, or liqueur, in the proportion of one tablespoon of
vanilla sugar or orange rind, and one liqueur-glass of liqueur, to
the quantities given above), twelve oz. of sifted flour, and eight oz.
of melted butter, the latter being carefully poured into the paste
without allowing it to bubble. Mix these ingredients with the paste,
raising the latter with a spatula that it may not get heavy.

Bake it in buttered and floured moulds.

Remarks.—A preparation of Biscuit— (sponge cake) or *Génoise*
reaches the *"ribbon" stage* when it becomes thick, draws out in rib-
bon-form, and takes some time to level itself again when a spoon is
pulled out of it. This state of the paste is also indicative of its
lightness.

2377—ORDINARY GENOISE PASTE FOR CUTTING UP

Pâte à Genoise Ordinaire

Quantities.—One lb. of sugar, twelve eggs, thirteen oz. of flour,
eight oz. of butter, and the quantity of flavoring thought sufficient.

Proceed exactly as in the preceding recipe, in everything pertaining to the working of the paste.

This paste is baked in buttered and paper lined pans, in which
it is spread in layers one and one-quarter inches thick, that it may
rise to about one and three-quarter inches thick, while baking.

2378—LADY FINGERS SPONGE PASTE   *Pâte pour Biscuits à la Cuiller*

Stir one lb. of sugar and sixteen egg-yolks in a bowl until the
preparation has whitened slightly and has reached the *ribbon* stage.
Now add a tablespoon of orange-flower water; mix with twelve oz.
of sifted flour, followed by sixteen egg-whites, beaten to a stiff froth.
Take care to cut in the whites with the spatula, that they may remain quite light.

To Shape the Fingers.—Put the paste, little by little, into a canvas
pastry-bag, fitted with a plain tube of one-half inch flat opening.
Close the bag; pipe the biscuits on sheets of strong paper; sprinkle

them with powdered sugar, and shake off any superfluous sugar by holding the sheets end upwards.

Sprinkle a few drops of water upon the biscuits by means of a moistened brush to aid the beading of the sugar, and remember that a very moderate oven is the best for the completion of this beading.

2379—SAVOY SPONGE PASTE   *Pâte pour Biscuit de Savoie*

Stir one lb. of sugar and fourteen egg-yolks in a bowl until the preparation reaches the *ribbon stage*. Flavor with vanilla sugar; add six oz. of very dry, sifted flour mixed with six oz. of cornstarch, and finally cut in the fourteen egg-whites, which should be beaten very stiff.

Carefully set the preparation in buttered and cornstarch-dredged moulds, filling the latter only two-thirds full, and leaving the remaining third to be filled by the rising of the paste while baking.

Bake in a regular, moderate oven.

2380—SPONGE BISCUIT PASTE   *Pâte à Biscuit Manqué*

Stir one lb. of sugar with eighteen egg-yolks in a bowl until the preparation is white and light. Add three tablespoons of rum, thirteen oz. of sifted flour, and ten oz. of melted butter, carefully poured into the mixture. Mix, raising the paste from the bottom of the bowl with the spatula.

Put the preparation in special buttered and floured moulds, filling the latter only two-thirds full. Bake in a moderate oven.

2381—PUNCH BISCUIT SPONGE PASTE   *Pâte à Biscuit Punch*

Stir one lb. of sugar, twelve egg-yolks, and three eggs in a bowl, until the whole becomes frothy. Flavor with a bare tablespoon of orange sugar, the same amount of lemon sugar, and three tablespoons of best rum, and add twelve oz. of sifted flour, ten oz. of melted butter, and the whites of eight eggs beaten to a stiff froth. Mix with the usual precautions, that the paste may not be heavy.

Bake the preparation in buttered moulds, in paper cases or in rings, according to the purpose it is intended for. Use a moderate oven.

2382—ORDINARY MERINGUE   *Meringue Ordinaire*

Whisk the whites of eight eggs until they are as stiff as it is possible to make them. Sprinkle them with one lb. of powdered sugar, and mix them with the latter carefully, that they may retain all their lightness.

2383a—ITALIAN STYLE MERINGUE   *Meringue à l'Italienne*

Cook one lb. of sugar to the *large-ball* stage, and meanwhile whisk the whites of eight eggs to a stiff froth, so as to have them ready simultaneously with the sugar.

Pour the cooked sugar into the egg-whites, slowly and without stopping, and mix up briskly with the wire whisk.

2384b—ITALIAN STYLE MERINGUE   *Meringue à l'Italienne*

Mix one lb. of very best powdered sugar and the whites of eight eggs in a copper bowl. Place the utensil on hot cinders or on the side of the stove, that the preparation may be lukewarm while in progress.

Whisk the meringue until it is of sufficient consistency to span the wires of the whisk. If it is not to be used at once, transfer the paste to a small bowl; cover it with a round piece of paper, and set it in a cool place.

2385—ALMOND PASTE   *Pâte d'Amandes*

Instead of the antiquated and difficult method of making almond pastes in the mortar, a crushing machine is now used which not only yields a much smoother paste, but also greatly simplifies the work. Almond paste, which consists of almonds, sugar, and egg-whites, in quantities varying in accordance with the purpose of the paste, is now sold ready-made. It has only to be finished with a little sugar, white of egg, and other ingredients, subject to the use to which it is to be put.

2386—MELTING ALMOND PASTE (FOR STUFFING AND IMITATING FRUIT)   *Pâte d'Amandes Fondante*

Pass eight oz. of dry, skinned almonds through the grinder.

Place them in the mortar, together with the selected flavoring *essence;* either a tablespoon of vanilla sugar or a small glass of liqueur; and add to them, little by little, working the while with the pestle, one lb. of sugar cooked to the *small-crack* stage.

With this general recipe, the melting paste may be varied at will by an increase or decrease in the quantity of sugar.

2387—PISTACHIOS *Pistaches*

These should belong to the pastry-cook's stock, but, as a rule, they are only prepared just before being served. To skin them, proceed as in the case of almonds (2338).

2388—PISTACHIO PASTE FOR INFUSIONS
Pâte de Pistaches pour Infusions

As soon as the pistachios are skinned, washed, and dried, crush them in the mortar to a very smooth paste, which set in boiled milk, to infuse.

As the color of pistachios is weak, it is strengthened in preparations containing them with a few drops of vegetable green, while its aroma is thrown into relief with a drop of vanilla.

2389—MELTING PISTACHIO PASTE *Pâte de Pistaches Fondante*

Put seven oz. of pistachios and two oz. of almonds through the grinder; both should have been just skinned. Put the paste into the mortar; add to it two tablespoons of syrup, strongly flavored with vanilla, followed by eight oz. of sugar, cooked to the *small-crack* stage, and added to the paste little by little.

Transfer the paste to a marble slab, and finish it by combining three tablespoons of icing sugar with it.

THE PREPARATION AND COOKING OF VARIOUS PASTRY CRUSTS USED IN COOKERY

2390—VOL-AU-VENT CRUST *Croûte de Vol-au-Vent*

Prepare the puff-paste as directed under (2366). Make the layer of paste of an even thickness of four-fifths inch; set on it an overturned plate or a saucepan-lid, the size of which should be that intended for the Vol-au-vent, and cut the paste obliquely, following round the edges of the lid or plate with a small knife. Turn the layer of paste over, and set it on a slightly moistened round baking sheet; groove it all round; brush it with egg, and describe a circle on top of it with the point of a knife, not cutting deeply, one and one-quarter inches away from the edge, to form the cover of the Vol-au-vent. Streak this cover criss-cross-fashion; also streak the body of the Vol-au-vent with the point of a small knife, and bake it in a rather hot oven.

Upon taking the Vol-au-vent from the oven, remove its cover, and clear it of the soft part of the paste which will be found on the inside.

2391—SMALL-PATTY CRUSTS *Croûte de Bouchées*

Bouchées are really small Vol-au-vents. Roll out the paste, making it a good one-third inch thick. Cut this layer with a grooved round cutter three inches in diameter; set the rounds of stamped-out paste on a moistened pan; brush with egg, and make a circular incision in each of them, one-half inch from their edges, either with the point of a small knife or with an even, round cutter dipped in hot water. But do not cut all the way down.

Bake in a hot oven, and remove the insides of the bouchées on taking them out of the oven. "Mignonnes Bouchées," which are used as a garnish, are stamped out with a round cutter two inches in diameter, and are slightly thicker than ordinary bouchées.

2392—SMALL HOT PATTIES *Croûte de Bouchées Mignonnes*

Roll out the puff-paste (2366) to a thickness of one-sixth inch, and stamp it out with an even round cutter three inches in diameter. With the trimmings from this operation, rolled somewhat more thinly, make an equal quantity of rounds, and lay them on a pan. Slightly moisten the edges of these rounds with a brush; fill their centers with some *forcemeat*, rolled to the size of a hazel-nut; cover the *forcemeat* with the rounds stamped out from the first; press upon these with the back of a round cutter two inches in diameter; brush them with egg, and bake them in a hot oven for twelve or fourteen minutes.

2393—TARTLET CRUSTS *Croûtes de Tartelettes*

For *tartlet crusts*, which are put to various uses, take either even or fluted, large or small moulds, subject to the requirements.

Roll out a piece of short paste (2356) to a thickness of one-fifth inch; stamp it out with a fluted or scalloped round cutter of a size in proportion to the moulds used; line the buttered moulds with these rounds of paste; pierce the paste on the bottom of each with the point of a small knife; line with good-quality paper; fill up with lentils, split peas, or rice, just to keep the form, and bake in a moderate oven. When the paste is baked, remove the dry vegetable used and the paper, and place the crusts in the warming-oven, that they may be quite dry; or brush with egg inside, and set them in the front of the oven for a few minutes.

2394—TIMBALE CRUST *Croûte de Timbale*

Butter a *Charlotte-mould,* and decorate its sides with some sort of design made from noodle-paste trimmings to which a little powdered sugar has been added. Shape a piece of short paste (2356), of a size in proportion to the mould, like a ball; roll it out to a disc; sprinkle it with flour, and fold it in two. Draw the ends gently towards the center, so as to form a kind of skullcap, and take care to not crease the paste. Make this skullcap of an even thickness of one-third inch, and place it in the mould.

Press it well upon the bottom and sides of the mould, that it may acquire the shape of the latter; line the mould inside with good buttered paper; fill up with lentils or split peas, just to keep the form, letting them project in a dome above the edges of the paste, and cover with a round sheet of paper.

Prepare a round layer of paste, one-fifth inch thick, a little larger diametrically than the *timbale* one. Slightly moisten the inside edges of the *timbale;* cover it with the prepared disc of paste, and seal it well down to the edges of the *timbale,* pressing it between the fingers in such a way as to form an edge reaching one-half inch beyond the brim of the mould all round.

Pinch this edge with paste-pincers inside and out.

With a round or oval grooved fancy-cutter stamp out some imitation leaves from a very thin layer of paste, and imitate the veins of the leaves with the back of a knife; or stamp out some triangles of paste; shape them like leaves, and set these (slightly overlapping one another) upon the dome of the *timbale* in superimposed rows.

Finish with three rounds of paste, stamped out with a grooved round cutter of a different size from the first, and make a hole in the center of each roundel with a round, even fancy-cutter. Brush with egg and bake in a moderate oven. When the outside of the *timbale* is well browned, detach and remove the cover formed by the leaves. Remove the split peas and the paper; brush with egg the inside of the *timbale,* and leave it to dry in the front of the oven or in the warming-oven.

2395—CRUST FOR DEEP PIES   *Croûte de Flan*

With short or any other kind of paste prepare a layer one-sixth inch thick, the diameter of which should be one-fourth as long again as that of the spring-form used. Lift this layer, and place it into the previously-buttered spring-form, pressing it with the fingers, that it may assume the shape of the mould. Then roll the rolling-pin across the top of the rim, so that the overlapping paste may be cut away; press the thickness of paste that has been formed at the top between the fingers in such a way as to make it project above the edges of the form, and make a regular edge. Pinch this edge with the pastry pincers, and set the spring-form on a round baking sheet.

Prick it with the point of a small knife; line the bottom and sides with slightly-buttered, white paper; fill the pastry with dry lentils or split peas, just to keep the form, and bake in a moderately hot oven for about twenty-five minutes.

Then remove the lentils and paper, as also the spring-form rim, and return the crust to the oven for a few minutes to brown, if it is not already sufficiently colored.

If the paste be required very dry, place the crust in the warming-oven for a little while, or brush the inside with egg, and set it in the front of the oven for a few minutes.

2396—THE LINING AND COVERING OF RAISED AND DRESSED PIES
Croûtes pour les "Pies"

The moulds for raised pies are oval or round. If they are round, make a layer of patty paste, one-half inch thick, in proportion to the size of the mould. (Deep dish pie mould.)

Sprinkle this paste with flour, fold it in two, and shape it like a skullcap, after the manner described under *"Timbale Crust"* (2394). It is only necessary to press this skullcap of paste into the buttered mould in order to give it the shape of the latter. If the mould is oval, proceed in the same way, giving the skullcap an oval shape.

When the raised pie is filled, first cover the filling with a some-what thin, round, or oval layer of paste, in accordance with the shape of the mould, and seal it well down upon the moistened edges. Then cut away the superfluous paste of the edge, so as to make the latter even and neat, and pinch it outside and in. Raised pies are covered in two ways—either with a layer of puff-paste (2366), or with leaves of paste stamped out with a round cutter or a knife, the veins being imitated with the back of a knife.

In the first case, prepare a layer of puff-paste one-third inch thick, equal in size to the inside of the patty. Place this layer of paste upon the cover of the pie, after having slightly moistened it; brush with egg and decorate with lines made by back of knife, and make a slit in the top for the escape of steam.

In the second case, prepare the paste leaves as directed above, and lay them on the pie (slightly overlapping one another) in super-imposed rows, starting from the bottom. On the top of the pie set three or four scalloped rounds of paste, graduated in size, and stuck one upon the other, each round having a hole in its center for the escape of steam.

Brush with egg and set the pie in the oven.

The baking of raised pies made with raw *forcemeat* is done in a moderately-heated oven. Bear in mind that the larger the pie is, the more moderate should be the oven.

VARIOUS CUSTARDS

HOT CUSTARDS

2397—ENGLISH CREAM　　　　　　　　　　*Crème Anglaise*

This custard permits of various methods of preparation which are subject to the purpose for which it is intended. It is the chief sauce for entremets (sweet dishes), and whether it be *poached* in a deep dish or in a mould, it constitutes one of the oldest and best-known desserts. This last kind of custard will be examined hereafter. At present I shall only deal with the variety used either as a sauce or an accompaniment, cold or hot. It is extremely difficult to prescribe fixed quantities for this custard, for the former depend a great deal upon the diners' tastes, and, whereas some like a thick custard, others go to the extreme of wishing it just liquid enough to be drunk like any other beverage.

The quantities given below are suited to a custard of medium consistency, but if a thicker custard were desired, the number of egg-yolks would have to be proportionately increased, and *vice-versa*.

The quantity of sugar also varies, subject to the diners' tastes, and, as the amount used (except in the case of unreasonable excess) does not affect the consistency of the custard, it may be graduated from three to ten or twelve oz. per quart, as taste may dictate. Six oz. of sugar per quart of milk constitutes a happy medium.

English custard permits of all the flavoring *essences* used for desserts, but the one which suits it best is vanilla. When this last-named flavor or that of filberts, almond *pralin,* or coffee is used, it is well to put the required quantity to infuse for twenty minutes in the boiling milk, after the latter has been measured. Chocolate is first melted and then gradually added to the custard before it is cooked. Other *aromatic essences* or liqueurs are added to the custard after it has been strained.

English custard permits of two methods of preparation:—

Recipe A.—Put twelve raw egg-yolks and three-quarters lb. of powdered sugar in a bowl. Mix the sugar a little with the yolks, and beat the latter with a beater until they have entirely absorbed the sugar, and the resulting mixture is white and has reached the *ribbon* stage (2376). Then pour one quart of boiling milk into the egg mixture, little by little, mixing the whole with a whisk. Then put the preparation on the fire, stirring it with a spatula, and cook it until it approaches the boil and properly coats the spoon. Take care not to let it boil, for this would separate the preparation. In any case, when the sauce is intended for hot sweets, by adding a tablespoon of arrowroot or cornstarch, it may be prevented from separating.

When the custard is cooked, as already explained, strain it, either through a strainer, into a *bain-marie* (water-bath), if it is to be served hot, or through a sieve into a large, enamelled bowl, where it should be frequently stirred to be kept smooth while cooling.

Custard prepared in this way forms the base of all ice creams, of which I shall speak later on. It may serve as an addition to all cold or hot desserts which call for a sauce. When, while it is still lukewarm, it is combined with its weight of best butter, it constitutes the delicious butter cream, which is the richest and most delicate of the pastry-cook's confections.

Finally, if about four oz. of dissolved gelatine per quart of cooled milk be added to it, and it be mixed with twice its volume of whipped cream, it represents the preparation for Bavarian Creams and Russian Charlottes.

Recipe B.—Dissolve six oz. of sugar in one quart of milk; boil, and pour the mixture, little by little, over twelve egg-yolks, whisking the latter briskly the while. When this custard is to be moulded, or is intended for a Cabinet Pudding, or some other similar preparation, which must be finally *poached,* strain it as soon as it is mixed, without cooking it.

If, on the other hand, it is intended for an accompaniment, or for the preparation of butter creams or ices, cook it as directed in Recipe A.

2398—ENGLISH CUSTARD (TO ACCOMPANY COLD OR HOT STEWED FRUIT) *Crème Anglaise pour Compôtes*

For this purpose English custard (2397) is made from only ten egg-yolks per quart of milk. Serve it in shallow silver or porcelain dishes; sprinkle its surface copiously with *icing sugar* (2346a), and criss-cross it with a red-hot iron.

2399—FRANGIPAN CREAM *Crème Frangipan*

As in the case of English custard (2397), Frangipan custard varies in the quantities of its ingredients in accordance with its purpose and personal taste. The recipe given below is an average one, which the cook will be able to modify, in regard to consistency, by increasing or decreasing the amount of flour.

Mix one-half lb. of powdered sugar, two oz. of flour, two whole eggs, and the yolks of five in a bowl. Pour one pint of boiling milk over this paste, stirring it briskly the while; add a few grains of salt and the selected flavoring, and set the saucepan on the fire, that the *Frangipan* may cook. Do not cease stirring this cream while it is cooking, for it burns easily. (A double boiler might be useful here.)

Let it boil a few minutes; pour it into a bowl, and combine three oz. of fresh butter and two tablespoons of dry, crushed macaroons with it. When the whole is well mixed, smooth the surface of the custard with a well-buttered spoon, so that no crust may form while the cooling progresses.

2400—FRANGIPAN FOR FRIED CREAM *Frangipan pour Crèmes Frites*

Proceed as above, but so apportion the quantities as to obtain a very firm cream. The quantities should be as follows:—Six oz. of flour, six oz. of sugar, ten egg-yolks, four whole eggs, one quart of milk, and one oz. of butter.

When this cream is cooked, spread it in a layer one inch thick on a buttered tray or on a marble slab; carefully butter its surface, and let it cool before using it.

COLD CUSTARDS

2401—PASTRY CREAM *Crème St. Honoré*

Mix one lb. of powdered sugar with four oz. of flour and twelve egg-yolks, and dilute with one quart of boiling milk. Cook this cream, stirring it continually the while; and, as soon as it boils, add to it a few drops of orange-flower water and about two oz. of dissolved gelatine, softened in cold water. Boil the cream a few minutes; take it off the fire, and, while stirring it briskly, carefully combine with it twelve egg-whites, beaten to a stiff froth.

N.B.—Some chefs call this St. Honoré cream (for, as a matter of fact, it serves chiefly in the garnishing of sweet dishes bearing that name), and give the name of Pastry cream to the same preparation minus the egg-whites and the gelatine. I prefer to abide by the principle given above, and to consider the cream without whisked egg-whites merely as a *Frangipan*, with which it has many points in common.

Pastry cream may be flavored according to fancy. The addition of the gelatine is not necessary when the cream is to be served immediately, or when it only has a moment or two to wait. But it is indispensable to prevent the separation of the cream, especially in hot weather, if it has to wait at all.

2402—CHANTILLY WHIPPED CREAM   *Crème Chantilly*

Nothing could be simpler or more exquisite than this preparation, which is obtained by whipping the best cream (kept fresh for twenty-four hours in the refrigerator). The cream speedily increases in volume and becomes frothy. The operation should then be stopped, lest the cream turn to butter, and there should be immediately added to it four oz. of powdered sugar (part of which should be the vanilla kind) per quart, and then the preparation should be placed in a cool place until required.

N.B.—The addition of a little dissolved or powdered tragacanth gum or gelatine to the cream results in a more frothy cream being obtained, but the result is neither as fresh nor as perfect in taste when it is not combined with a sweet or ice preparation.

Various Preparations for Entremets

2403—PREPARATIONS FOR PANCAKES AND PANNEQUETS
Compositions pour Crêpes et Pannequets

Preparation A.—Put into a basin one lb. of sifted flour, six oz. of powdered sugar, and a pinch of salt. Dilute with ten eggs and one quart of milk, added by degrees. Flavor with one heaped tablespoon of orange, lemon or vanilla sugar, which should form part of the total weight of sugar prescribed; or with one-eighth pint of some liqueur such as brandy, kirsch, rum, etc., which should form part of the total liquid.

Preparation B.—Mix one lb. of flour, three and one-half oz. of powdered sugar and a pinch of salt, with nine eggs and a half-pint of cream. Add one-eighth pint of brandy, two and a half-oz. of melted butter and one and a half-pints of milk. Pass the whole through a fine strainer, and finish it with one-eighth pint of *orgeat* syrup or almond milk (2506) and three oz. of finely-crushed macaroons.

Preparation C.—Mix one lb. of flour, three and a half oz. of powdered sugar and a pinch of salt with nine eggs. Stir the mixture well; add to it a half-pint of fresh cream and one pint of milk. Finish with a half-pint of whipped cream, and flavor as taste may suggest.

Preparation D.—Mix one lb. of flour, three and a half oz. of powdered sugar and a pinch of salt, with five eggs and the yolks of three. Add one and three-quarter pints of milk and five egg-whites beaten to a stiff froth.

Flavor according to taste.

2404—RICE PREPARATION FOR DESSERTS   *Riz pour Entremets*

Wash one lb. of Southern or Indian rice; cover it with plenty of cold water; allow it to come to a boil, and drain it the moment it has boiled. Wash it once more in lukewarm water; drain it, and set it to cook with two pints of boiled milk, two-thirds lb. of sugar, a pinch of salt and three oz. of butter.

Flavor with a stick of vanilla or a few strips of orange or lemon rind, tied together with a thread. When the liquid begins to boil, cover the saucepan; place it in the oven, and let it cook gently for twenty or twenty-five minutes, without once touching the rice.

On taking it from the oven, thicken it with the yolks of sixteen eggs, which should be mixed with it by means of a fork in such a way as not to break the rice grains, which ought to remain whole.

N.B.—In some cases, the milk and the sugar may be replaced (for the cooking process) by an equal amount of sugar and water syrup at 12° (Saccharometer).

2405—SOUFFLE PREPARATIONS   *Compositions pour Soufflés*

Soufflé preparations are of two kinds:—

Those prepared with cream, which if necessary may serve for all *soufflés;* and those with a fruit-*purée* base, which permit of a more pronounced flavor for fruit *soufflés* than if these were prepared with cream.

Cream-soufflé Preparation for Four People.—Boil one-sixth pint of milk with one oz. of sugar; add a tablespoon of flour diluted in a little cold milk; cook for two minutes, and finish, away from the fire, with a piece of butter the size of a walnut, and two egg-yolks with three whites beaten to a stiff froth.

Soufflé Preparation for a Big Party.—Thoroughly mix a half-lb. of flour, a half-lb. of sugar, four eggs and the yolks of three, in a saucepan. Mix with one quart of boiling milk; add a stick of vanilla; boil, and cook for two minutes, stirring constantly.

Finish, away from the fire, with four oz. of butter, five egg-yolks, and twelve whites, beaten to a very stiff froth.

Soufflé Preparation with a Fruit Base.—Take one lb. of sugar cooked to the *small-crack* stage; add one lb. of the pulp or *purée* of the fruit to be used, and ten egg-whites, beaten to a stiff froth.

Proceed thus: Having cooked the sugar to the extent stated above, add to it the fruit pulp. If the latter reduces the sugar a stage or two, cook it again in order to return it to the *small-crack* stage; and, when this is reached, pour it over the whites.

Dishing and Cooking of Soufflés.—Whatever the soufflés may consist of, cook them in a *timbale,* or in a special false-bottomed dish, buttered and sugared inside. Cook in a somewhat moderate oven, that the heat may reach the center of the *soufflé* by degrees.

Two minutes before taking the *soufflé* from the oven, sprinkle it with *icing sugar,* which, when it becomes caramel upon the surface of the *soufflé,* constitutes the *glazing.*

The decoration of *soufflés* is optional, and, in any case, should not be overdone.

Hot Sauces for Desserts

2406—ENGLISH SAUCE *Sauce Anglaise*
See the Custard recipe (2397).

2407—CHOCOLATE SAUCE *Sauce au Chocolat*
Dissolve half-lb. of grated chocolate in two-thirds pint of water. Add a tablespoon of vanilla sugar; cook gently for twenty-five min-utes, and complete at the last moment with three tablespoons of cream and a piece of best butter, the size of a walnut.

2408—SABAYON *Sabayon*
Mix one lb. of powdered sugar with twelve egg-yolks, in a basin, until the mixture has whitened slightly. Dilute with one quart of dry, white wine; pour the whole in a narrow *bain-marie* (double-boiler), which should be placed in a receptacle containing boiling water, and whisk it until it is four times its former size, and is firm and frothy.

N.B.—Sabayon may also be made with milk instead of white wine, and it may be flavored according to taste.

2409—FRUIT SAUCE *Sauces aux Fruits*
Apricots, red-currants, greengages, and mirabelle (yellow) plums are the best fruits for sweet sauces. Other fruits, such as peaches,

Bartlet pears, apples, etc., may also be used in the form of light *purées* or *cullises*.

2410—APRICOT SAUCE   *Sauce à l'Abricot*

Rub some very ripe or stewed apricots through a sieve, and thin the *purée* with the required quantity of syrup at 28° (Saccharom.). Boil, skimming carefully the while; take off the fire when the sauce coats the spoon, and flavor according to taste.

If this sauce is to be used with pastry crusts, a little best butter may be added to it.

2411—RED CURRANT SAUCE   *Sauce Groseilles*

Melt some red currant jelly and flavor it with kirsch.

This sauce may be slightly thickened with arrowroot or cornstarch.

2412—ORANGE SAUCE   *Sauce à l'Orange*

Rub some orange marmalade through a sieve; add one-third of its bulk of apricot sauce, and flavor with Curaçao.

2413—HAZEL-NUT SAUCE   *Sauce Noisette*

Flavor some English custard (2397) with an infusion of grilled hazel-nuts, and add two tablespoons of moulded filbert *pralin* per quart of custard.

2414—GREENGAGE OR MIRABELLE SAUCE
Sauce aux Reines Claude ou Mirabelles

Proceed as for apricot sauce and flavor with kirsch.

2415—CHERRY SAUCE   *Sauce aux Cerises*

Take the syrup of some stewed cherries, add an equal quantity of red-currant jelly, and flavor with kirsch.

2416—RASPBERRY SAUCE   *Sauce aux Framboises*

Take the required quantity of melted raspberry jelly; thicken it slightly with arrowroot or cornstarch, and flavor with kirsch.

2417—STRAWBERRY SAUCE   *Sauce aux Fraises*

Proceed as for (2416).

2418—THICKENED SYRUPS   *Sirops Liés*

These accompaniments of desserts, which are commonly used in Germany, have this in their favor, that they are economical; but they should be used in moderation. To make them, take some sugar syrup at 15°, thickened with arrowroot, potato flour, or cornstarch, colored according to the purpose for which it is required, and flavored with some liqueur or *essence* at the last moment.

It is with this kind of sauce that custards and all other sorts of *tartlets* are coated in northern European countries.

HOT SWEET DISHES

FRITTERS

The numerous fritter recipes for desserts may all be grouped into five leading classes, viz.:—

(1) Fruit fritters.

(2) Custard fritters.

(3) Viennese fritters.

(4) Souffléd fritters.

(5) Many other fritters which are more or less like the four former ones without entirely resembling them.

2419—FRESH FRUIT AND FLOWER FRITTERS
Pâte de Beignets de Fruits et de Fleurs

Subject to the treatment undergone by them, fruits for fritters are of two kinds: firm fruits, such as apples and pears, and juicy fruits, such as strawberries, etc.

2420—FRITTERS OF FRUITS WITH FIRM PULPS, SUCH AS APRICOT FRITTERS
Beignet de Fruits à Pulpe Compacte

Select some apricots that are not over-ripe; cut them in two; sprinkle them with sugar, and set them to steep for an hour in kirsch, brandy, or rum, subject to taste. A few minutes before serving, dry the halved apricots, dip them in batter (234), and fry them in hot fat. Drain them on a napkin; set the fritters on a pan; cover them with icing sugar, and *glaze* them in a hot oven or at the *salamander* or under a hot broiler flame. Place them on a napkin, and serve them at once.

N.B.—Proceed in precisely the same way for apple, pear, peach, or banana fritters.

2421—JUICY FRUIT FRITTERS, SUCH AS STRAWBERRY FRITTERS
Beignets de Fruits Aqueux

Select some large, somewhat firm strawberries; sugar them copiously; sprinkle them with kirsch, and let them steep on ice for thirty minutes.

It is most essential that the strawberries be well sugared before soaking, because the heat of the fat sours them while the fritters are being fried, and they consequently become tart.

A few minutes before serving, drain the strawberries, dip them in batter (234), and plunge them into very hot fat. Drain them, place them on lace paper, and sprinkle them with icing sugar, by means of a shaker.

N.B.—The procedure is the same for Raspberry, Red-currant, Cherry, Orange, and Tangerine fritters. For the last-named, it is better to quarter them and peel them raw, than to slice them.

2422—BLOSSOM FRITTERS, SUCH AS ACACIA-FLOWER FRITTERS
Beignets de Fleurs d'Acacia

Select some full-blown acacia flowers; sprinkle them with sugar and liqueur brandy, and leave them to steep for thirty minutes.

Dip them in batter (234); plunge them into plenty of hot fat; drain them; sprinkle them with sugar and serve them on a napkin.

N.B.—Proceed as above for Elder-Blossom, Lily, and Vegetable-Blossom fritters; but in the case of the last two, the quartered crowns of the flowers, alone, are used.

2423—CUSTARD FRITTERS OR FRIED CREAM   *Beignets de Crème*

Custard fritters may be prepared in the three following totally different ways.

1st Method.—Cut up preparation (2400) with a round, square, or diamond-shaped fancy cutter, as taste may dictate. Treat the resulting pieces of custard twice *à l'anglaise,* using very fine and fresh bread-crumbs for the purpose. Press upon the bread-crumbs with the blade of a knife that they may adhere properly, and fry the pieces of custard cream in very hot fat. On taking the fritters out of the fat sprinkle them with icing sugar, and serve them on a napkin.

N.B.—Instead of treating these fritters *à l'anglaise,* they may be dipped into batter and treated as directed in the case of Apricot fritters (2420).

2nd Method.—Prepare a custard as for a "crème renversée" (2639), using only whole eggs, that it may be firm; and *poach* it in a pan of a shape which will facilitate the cutting-up of the preparation. When the latter is quite cool, cut it up as fancy may suggest; dip the pieces in batter (234) and plunge them in plenty of hot fat. Drain them on a piece of linen or absorbent paper; sprinkle them with icing sugar; *glaze* them in a hot oven, and serve them on a napkin.

3rd Method.—Prepare some regular-shaped hollow *meringues,* and keep them very dry.

When they have cooled, open them slightly on top, and, through the hole in each, fill them either with a Bavarian cream preparation (2622), with some kind of ice-cream, or with a fruit *salpicon* thickened with stewed apricots or plums. Close the holes with the pieces that were cut out, and place the *meringues* in the refrigerator for an hour.

When about to serve them, quickly treat them *à l'anglaise;* set them (opened side uppermost) in a frying-basket, and dip them for a few seconds in smoking fat. Take them out as soon as their crusts have acquired a golden color; sprinkle them with icing sugar; place them on a napkin, and serve them immediately.

2424—VIENNESE FRITTERS *Beignets Viennois*

Quantities for the paste of Viennese fritters: one lb. of flour; six oz. of butter; half oz. of yeast; five eggs; half oz. of salt; two-third oz. of sugar; and one-sixth pint of milk. This paste is prepared exactly like Brioche paste (2368).

In any case, as it has to be worked with the rolling-pin, always keep it a little firm.

2425—HOT VIENNESE FRITTERS *Beignets Viennois Chauds*

Roll out a piece of the paste given above to a thickness of one-fifth inch.

Spread upon it, at regular intervals, small quantities (about the size of a large walnut) either of stewed fruit or jam. Moisten slightly; cover with a second layer of paste, of the same size and thickness as the former; press upon it with the back of a round cutter, so as to ensure the joining of the two layers of paste, and then stamp the whole out with an even cutter two and a half inches in diameter.

Set the fritters on a pan covered with a flour-dusted piece of linen; let the paste rise for thirty minutes, and then fry them in plenty of hot fat. Drain them; sprinkle them with icing sugar and serve them on a napkin.

N.B.—These fritters may be accompanied by frothy sauces, flavored with vanilla, lemon, orange, coffee, or kirsch, etc., the type of which is the Sabayon with cream (2408).

2426—COLD VIENNESE FRITTERS   *Beignets Viennois Froids*
Roll out a piece of the paste prescribed, which should be kept somewhat soft, and stamp it out with a round cutter two and a half inches in diameter. Set half of these rounds of paste on buttered sheets of paper, lying on trays; fill them either with stewed fruit or jam; slightly moisten their edges; cover them with the remaining rounds of paste, and let the paste rise for thirty minutes.

A few minutes before serving, grasp the ends of the sheets of paper; plunge the fritters into plenty of hot fat, and take out the sheets of paper as soon as the fritters fall from them.

Drain them as soon as they begin to brown; and plunge them immediately into a light, hot syrup, flavored as fancy may dictate. Take them out as soon as they begin to be saturated, and serve them cold.

N.B.—In the case of either of these two methods of serving Viennese fritters, the latter, which are served under the name of "fritters à la Dauphine," may be garnished with fruit *salpicons* or cream preparations.

SOUFFLÉ FRITTERS

2427—ORDINARY SOUFFLE FRITTERS   *Beignets Soufflés Ordinaires*
Put one pint of water, three and a half oz. of butter, a pinch of salt and two pinches of sugar into a saucepan. Boil; take the utensil off the fire in order to add two-thirds lb. of sifted flour, and mix up the whole. Then dry this paste as directed for *pâte à choux* or cream puff paste (2373); and finish it, away from the fire, with seven eggs, added one by one.

Flavor according to taste.

Take this paste in portions, the size of small walnuts; put these portions in moderately hot fat, and gradually increase the heat of the latter, so as to ensure the rising of the paste.

When the fritters are quite dry outside, drain them; serve them on a napkin, and sprinkle them with icing sugar (2346a).

2428—SURPRISE SOUFFLE FRITTERS   *Beignets Soufflés en Surprise*
Prepare the fritters exactly like the preceding ones. When taking them out of the fat, slit open slightly and fill them, by means of the

pastry-bag, either with stewed fruit, jam, a very fine, thickened *salpicon* of fruit, or some kind of cream, especially *frangipan* or pastry cream (2399).

VARIOUS FRITTERS

2429—FAVORITE PINEAPPLE FRITTERS   *Beignets d'Ananas Favorite*

Cut the pineapple into slices, one-third inch thick; cut each slice in two; sprinkle the half-discs with sugar and kirsch, and let them steep for thirty minutes. Then dry them and dip them into a very thick and almost cold *frangipan cream* (2399), combined with chopped pistachios. Set the cream-coated slices on a tray, and let them cool completely.

A little while before serving, take the slices from the tray; dip them in somewhat thin batter, and fry them in plenty of hot fat.

Drain them; sprinkle them with icing sugar; *glaze* them in a hot oven, and serve them on a napkin.

2430—FRITTERS A LA BOURGEOISE   *Beignets à la Bourgeoise*

Cut a stale brioche crown into slices, one-third inch thick, and dip these into fresh, sugared cream, flavored according to taste. Drain them; dry them slightly; dip them into thin batter, and fry them in very hot fat.

Drain them; sprinkle them with sugar, and serve them on a napkin.

2431—SYLVANA FRITTERS   *Beignets Sylvana*

Hollow out some small round brioches (2368), preserving the crusts for covers, and dip them in some thin, sugared and flavored fresh cream. Then fill them with a small fruit *salpicon* (filling) with kirsch; cover this with the reserved covers; dip them into thin batter, and fry them in plenty of hot fat.

Drain them; set them on a napkin, and sprinkle them with icing sugar.

2432—FRITTERS "A LA GRAND'MERE"   *Beignets Grand'Mère*

Spread upon a moistened pan a layer half-inch thick of very reduced, stewed fruit. Cut it up according to fancy; dip the pieces in batter (234), and fry them in plenty of hot fat.

On taking the fritters from the fat, sprinkle them with icing sugar and set them to *glaze* in a hot oven.

2433—REGINA FRITTERS *Beignets Regina*

Shape some lady-finger paste (2378) into large half-balls, one and a half-inch in diameter; bake these in a moderate oven and cool them. Then hollow out these half-balls; fill them with apricot or some other jam; join them in pairs, and dip them so as to thoroughly soak them in some fresh cream flavored with maraschino.

Drain them; treat them *à l'anglaise* with very fine bread-crumbs, and fry them in plenty of hot fat.

Drain them; set them on a napkin, and sprinkle them with icing sugar.

2434—MIGNON FRITTERS *Beignets Mignon*

Proceed as above, but substitute for biscuit half-bails of soft macaroons, saturated with kirsch syrup. For the rest of the procedure, follow the method of (2433).

2435—SUZON FRITTERS *Beignets Suzon*

Make a preparation of "rice for desserts" (2404), and spread it in a thin layer upon a pan to cool. Divide it up into rounds three and a half inches in diameter; fill the center of these with very stiff fruit filling *(salpicon);* roll the rounds into balls, to enclose the *salpicon;* dip these balls into thin batter, and fry them in plenty of hot fat.

Drain them; place them on a napkin, and sprinkle them with powdered sugar.

CHARLOTTES

2436—APPLE CHARLOTTE **Charlotte de Pomme**

Copiously butter a quart *Charlotte-mould.* Fill its bottom with heart-shaped *croûtons* of bread slices, slightly overlapping one another; and garnish its sides with rectangles of bread of exactly the same height as the mould, and also slightly overlapping one another. The *croûtons* and the rectangles should be one-eighth inch thick, and ought to have been dipped in melted butter before taking their place in the mould.

Meanwhile, quarter twelve fine russet apples; peel, slice, and cook them in a saucepan with one oz. of butter, two tablespoons of powdered sugar, and half the rind of a lemon and a little cinnamon tied into a bundle.

When the apples are cooked, and reduced to a thick *purée,*

remove the bundle of lemon peel and cinnamon, and add three tablespoons of stewed apricots.

Fill up the mould with this mixture, and remember to mound the apples in a high dome above the mould; for it settles in cooking.

Bake in a good, moderate oven for from thirty to thirty-five minutes.

2437—APPLE CHARLOTTE EMILE GIRET
Charlotte de Pommes Emile Giret

Prepare the *Charlotte* as directed above (2436), but in a shallow mould.

When it is unmoulded on the dish, completely cover it with an even coat, half inch thick, of very firm pastry cream (2401), and take care not to spoil the shape of the *Charlotte*.

Sprinkle the cream copiously with icing sugar; then, with a red-hot iron, criss-cross the *Charlotte* regularly all round; pressing the iron upon the sugar-sprinkled cream.

Surround the base of the *Charlotte* with a row of beads made by means of the pastry-bag, from the same cream as that already used.

2438—VARIOUS CHARLOTTES
Charlottes Diverses

Charlottes may be made with pears, peaches, apricots, etc., after the same procedure as that directed under (2436). The most important point to be remembered in their preparation is that the stewed fruit used should be very thick; otherwise it so softens the shell of bread that the *Charlotte* collapses as soon as it is turned out.

It is no less important that the mould should be as full as possible of the preparation used; for, as already explained, the latter settles in the cooking process.

2439—REGENCE CREAM
Crème Régence

Saturate half a pound of Lady Fingers (2378) with Maraschino Kirsch, and then dip them into a quart of boiled milk. Rub them through a very fine sieve, and add eight eggs, ten egg-yolks, two-thirds pound of powdered sugar and a small pinch of salt. Pour the whole into a shallow, *Charlotte-mould,* and set to *poach* in a *bain-marie* (water-bath) for about thirty-five minutes.

Let the mould rest for a few minutes; turn out its contents on a dish and surround the base of the cream with a crown of stewed half-apricots, each filled with a preserved cherry. Coat the whole with an apricot syrup, flavored with Kirsch and Maraschino.

2440—MERINGUED CREAM   *Crème Meringuée*

Prepare some "Crème a la Régence" as above, and *poach* it in a buttered deep border-mould in a *bain-marie* (water-bath); turn it out on a dish, and fill the middle of the border with Italian *meringue* (2383), combined with a *salpicon* of preserved fruit, soaked in Kirsch.

Decorate the border by means of a pastry-bag, fitted with a fancy tube and filled with plain Italian *meringue,* without the fruit; and set to brown in a moderate oven.

Serve an orange-flavored English custard (2398) separately.

2441—VILLAGE CREAM   *Crème Village*

Saturate five ounces of dry sponge fingers with Kirsch and Anisette, and set them in a deep dish in layers, alternated with coatings of stewed, seasonable fruit, such as pears, apples, etc.

Cover the whole with the following preparation: one-half pound of powdered sugar mixed with eight eggs and the yolks of four, and diluted with one and three-quarter pints of milk. *Poach* in a *bain-marie* (water-bath), in the oven.

2442—CUSTARD PUDDING   *Le Custard Pudding*

Custard pudding is a form of the English custard mentioned under (2397).

The difference between the two is that for the former whole eggs are used instead of the yolks alone, and that it is prepared according to the second method only. The average quantities for the preparation are:

Six eggs and six ounces of sugar per quart of milk. The custard is cooked in small deep pie-dishes in a *bain-marie* (water-bath), which should be placed in the oven or in a steamer.

According to whether the custard be required milky or thick, the number of eggs is either lessened or increased. In regard to the sugar, the guide should be your taste. If necessary, it may be removed altogether, and saccharine or glycerine may be used in its stead, as is customary for diabetic patients.

Custard is generally flavored with vanilla, but any other flavor suited to sweets may be used with it.

PANCAKES. *(See preparations No. 2403.)*

2443—CONVENT PANCAKES   *Crêpes du Couvent*

Pour into a buttered and hot omelet-pan some preparation A, sprinkle on it some Bartlett pears, cut into small dice; cover the latter with some more preparation A; toss the pancake in order to turn it; sprinkle it with powdered sugar, place it òn a napkin and serve it sizzling hot.

2444—GEORGETTE PANCAKES   *Crêpes Georgette*
Proceed as for Convent pancakes (2443), but substitute for pear-dice some very thin slices of pineapple, soaked in Maraschino.

2445—GIL-BLAS PANCAKES   *Crêpes Gil-Blas*
Make the following preparation: stir three ounces of best butter in a bowl until it acquires the consistency of a cream. Mix with this three ounces of powdered sugar, three tablespoons of liqueur brandy, a piece of butter the size of a filbert, and a few drops of lemon juice. Make pancakes with preparation C (2403); spread the prepared butter upon them; fold each pancake twice, and serve on a napkin.

2446—NORMANDE PANCAKES   *Crêpes à la Normande*
Proceed as for *Convent Pancakes* (2443), but for the pear dice substitute fine slices of apple, previously *sautéd* in butter.

2447—PARISIENNE PANCAKES   *Crêpes à la Parisienne*
These are made from preparation B, and are ungarnished.

2448—PAYSANNE PANCAKES   *Crêpes à la Paysanne*
Make these from preparation B (the *orgeat* syrup and the macaroons being removed), and flavor with orange-flower water.

2449—RUSSIAN PANCAKES   *Crêpes à la Russe*
Add to preparation C, a quarter of its volume of broken wafers saturated with kümmel and liqueur brandy, and make as usual.

2450—SUZETTE PANCAKES   *Crêpes Suzette*
Make these from preparation A, flavored with curaçao and tangerine juice. Coat them, like Gil-Blas pancakes (2445), with softened brandied butter, flavored with curaçao and tangerine juice.

The pancakes are fried and kept warm, but not stacked on top of each other. Now use the flat pan of a large chafing dish. Have a moderate flame under pan, and allow it gradually to heat up. Rub six lumps of sugar over one lemon and one orange-rind until the sugar has well absorbed the rind. Dilute the sugar in one-half cup of orange juice. Allow to stand. Cream one-half cup of sweet butter with two tablespoons of sugar and chill. When ready to use let this melt in the hot pan and strain orange juice over it. Let this reduce to half and lift the pancakes into this, fold them over twice, and ladle the sauce over them. In the meanwhile mix one quarter cup Cointreau or

Curaçao with two tablespoons of rum or Benedictine and pour this over the pancakes, the last of all one-third cup of Brandy or Grand Marnier. When this has heated up, which is essential, tilt the pan to the flame so the sauce catches fire, and stir the pancakes in this flaming sauce. Serve on heated plates while the sauce is still flaming.

CROQUETTES AND CRUSTS

2451—CHESTNUT CROQUETTES   *Croquettes de Marrons*

Peel the chestnuts after one of the ways directed (2172), and cook them in a thin syrup, flavored with vanilla. Reserve one small, whole chestnut for each *croquette*. Rub the remainder through a sieve; dry the *purée* over a hot fire, and thicken it with five egg-yolks and one and a half oz. of butter per lb. of *purée*. Let it cool.

Then divide the preparation up into portions the size of pigeons' eggs, and roll these portions into balls, with a chestnut in the center of each. Treat them *a l'anglaise* (174), with some very fine bread-crumbs; fry them in some very hot fat, and serve them on a napkin.

Serve a vanilla-flavored apricot sauce, separately.

2452—RICE CROQUETTES   *Croquettes de Riz*

Make a preparation as directed under (2404). Divide it up into two-oz. portions, moulded to the shape of such fruit as pears, apples, apricots, etc.; treat these *à l'anglaise* (174), like the Chestnut *Croquettes* (2451), and fry them in the same way. Serve an apricot sauce or a vanilla-flavored Sabayon (2408) separately.

2453—VARIOUS CROQUETTES   *Croquettes Diverses*

Croquettes may also be made from tapioca, semolina, vermicelli or fresh noodles (2291), etc., in which case the procedure is that of the Rice Croquettes (2452).

The preparation may be combined with currants and sultana raisins, and the *croquettes* are served with any suitable sauce.

2454—CRUSTS WITH FRUITS   *Croûte aux Fruits*

Cut some slices one-fifth inch thick from a stale Savarin (2371), which has not been moistened with syrup, and allow two for each person. Set these slices on a pan; sprinkle them with *icing sugar,* and put them in the oven so as to dry and *glaze* them at the same time. Arrange them in a circle round a bed of fried bread-crusts, and between each lay a slice of pineapple of exactly the same size as the cake slices.

Upon this crown of *croûtons,* set some quartered apples and some stewed pears. The pears may be stewed in a pinkish syrup, which by varying the color, makes the crust better looking.

Decorate with preserved cherries, angelica cut in diamond shapes, quartered yellow and green preserved kumquats, etc. Fix a small, peeled and white or pink pear on the top of the bed, by means of an ornamental skewer, coat with apricot sauce, flavored with Kirsch.

2455—CRUSTS LYONNAISE   *Croûte à la Lyonnaise*

Prepare the crusts as described above, and coat them with a smooth chestnut *purée*, flavored with vanilla; then, cover them with an apricot *purée*, cooked to the *small-thread* (215° F.) stage; sprinkle with finely-slivered and slightly-browned almonds, and arrange in a circle.

Fill the middle of the circle with chestnuts cooked in syrup, and seeded Malaga raisins, currants, and sultana raisins (washed and plumped in tepid water); the whole combined with an apricot *purée* thinned with a few tablespoons of Malaga wine.

2456—CRUSTS WITH MADEIRA   *Croûte au Madère*

Arrange the *glazed* crusts in a circle as already described (2454). Pour into their midst a filling consisting of equal parts of seeded, Malaga raisins, currants, and sultana raisins, plumped in tepid water and moistened with a Madeira-flavored, apricot syrup.

2457—CRUSTS A LA MARECHALE   *Croûte à la Maréchale*

Cut from a stale *mousseline brioche* (2369), some triangles of the same thickness as the ordinary crusts. Coat them with *pralin* (2352), and then set them on a pan; sprinkle them with sugar *glaze*, and dry the *pralin* in a moderate oven.

Place a bed of fried-bread slices four inches high on a dish, and surround it with a *salpicon* of pineapple, raisins, cherries, and crystallized orange-rind, mixed with some stiff stewed apples, combined with a little apricot *purée*. Set the pralin-coated triangles upright alongside of the *salpicon*, and surround them with a border of halved pears, stewed in syrup, half their quantity being white and the other pink.

On the top of the bread, set a small pear, cooked in pink syrup, fixed with a small ornamental skewer, and surround the border of halved pears with a band of apricot *purée*, flavored slightly with vanilla, and serve a sauceboat of the same *purée* separately.

2458—CRUSTS A LA NORMANDE   *Croûte à la Normande*

Prepare the crusts as indicated under (2454), coat them with very stiffly stewed apples, and arrange them in a circle.

Fill their center with stewed apples, prepared as for a *Charlotte* (2436), and upon the apples set a pyramid of quartered white and pink apples, cooked in syrup. Cover with reduced apple syrup, thickened with a little very smooth stewed apples flavored with Kirsch or cold rum.

2459—CRUSTS A LA PARISIENNE   *Croûte à la Parisienne*

Coat the crusts with *pralin,* as explained under (2457), and arrange them in a circle. In their midst set some thin slices of pineapple, the ends of which should rest upon the circle of crusts; in the middle, pour a filling of various fruits, mixed with an apricot *purée,* flavored with Madeira, and coat the circle of crusts with apricot syrup flavored with Madeira.

2460—CRUSTS WITH APRICOTS IN MARASCHINO
Croûte aux Abricots au Marasquin

Bake some *Savarin paste* (2371) in buttered *tartlet moulds.* When these *tartlets* are cooked, hollow them out at the top taking care to leave a somewhat thick border all round.

Coat them inside with *pralin* (2352), and dry them in a moderate oven. Then garnish the center of the *tartlets* with *frangipan cream* (2399), combined with filbert *pralin.* Upon this cream set a pitted apricot *poached* in Maraschino.

Surround the apricot with small, candied half-cherries, alternated with diamonds of angelica. Serve an apricot sauce, flavored with Maraschino, separately.

2461—CRUSTS VICTORIA   *Croûte Victoria*

Prepare a crust after (2456), and fill the center with candied cherries and *glazed* chestnuts. Serve an apricot sauce flavored with rum, separately.

OMELETS

Sweet omelets may be divided into four distinct classes, which are:—

1. Liqueur omelets
2. Jam omelets
3. *Souffléd* omelets
4. Surprise omelets

OMELETS WITH LIQUEUR

2462—OMELET WITH RUM   *Omelette au Rum*

Season the omelet (492) with sugar and a little salt, and cook it in the usual way. Set it on a long dish, sprinkle it with sugar and heated rum, and light the rum on bringing it to the table.

Jam Omelets

2463—APRICOT OMELET   *Omelette à l'Abricot*

Season the omelet as above, and, when about to roll it up, fill it inside with two tablespoons of apricot jam per six eggs. Set on a long dish; sprinkle with *icing sugar* (2436a), and either criss-cross the surface with a red-hot iron or *glaze* the omelet at the *salamander* or under a hot broiler flame.

2464—CHRISTMAS OMELET   *Omelette de Noël*

Beat the eggs with salt and sugar and add, per six eggs: two tablespoons of cream, a pinch of orange or lemon rind, and one tablespoon of rum. When about to roll up the omelet, garnish it copiously with mincemeat (2605), set it on a long dish; sprinkle it with heated rum, and light it at the table.

Souffléd Omelets

2465—SOUFFLE OMELET WITH VANILLA
Omelette Soufflée à la Vanille

Mix eight oz. of sugar and eight egg-yolks in a bowl, until the mixture has paled slightly, and draws up in ribbons when the spoon is pulled out of it. Add ten egg-whites, beaten to a very stiff froth, and mix the two preparations gently; cutting in and raising the whole with the spoon.

Set this preparation on a long, buttered and sugar-dusted dish, in the shape of an oval mound, and take care to put some of it aside in a pastry-bag.

Smooth it all round with the blade of a knife; decorate according to fancy with the contents of the pastry-bag, and cook in a good, moderate oven, for as long as the size of the omelet requires.

Two minutes before taking it from the oven, sprinkle it with *icing sugar*, that the latter, when melted, may cover the omelet with a glossy coat.

Flavor according to taste with vanilla, orange or lemon rind, rum, Kirsch, etc.; but remember to add the selected flavor to the preparation before the egg-whites are added to it.

SURPRISE OMELETS

2466—NORWEGIAN OMELET   *Omelette Norvègienne*

Place an oval bed of *Génoise* (2376) one and one-half in. thick upon a long dish, and let the bed be as long as the desired omelet. Upon it set a pyramid of ice-cream with fruit. Cover the ice-cream with ordinary *meringue* (2382); smooth it with a knife, making it of an even thickness of two-thirds of an inch in so doing; decorate it, by means of the pastry-bag, with the same *meringue,* and set in a very hot oven, that the *meringue* may cook and brown quickly, without the heat reaching the ice-cream inside.

2467—SURPRISE OMELET MYLORD   *Omelette en Surprise Mylord*

Proceed as directed above; but garnish the bed of *Génoise* with coatings of vanilla ice-cream, alternated with coatings of stewed pears. Cover with *meringue* (2382) and cook in the same way.

2468—TANGERINE SURPRISE OMELET
Omelette en Surprise aux Mandarines

The procedure is the same, but the vanilla ice-cream is replaced by tangerine ice. On taking the omelet out of the oven, surround it with tangerines *glazed* with sugar, cooked to the *large-crack* stage (248° F.).

2469—SURPRISE OMELET WITH CHERRIES
Omelette en Surprise aux Cerises

Garnish the bed of *Génoise* (2376) with red-currant ice (2768), flavored with raspberries and mixed with equal quantities of cherry ice (2764) and half-sugared cherries, steeped in Kirsch.

Finish it like the Norwegian Omelet (2466).

On taking it out of the oven, surround the omelet with drained cherries, preserved in brandy, sprinkle it with heated Kirsch, and fight at the table.

2470—SURPRISE OMELET MILADY, also called PEACH MILADY
Omelette en Surprise Milady

This is a surprise omelet, garnished with very firm raspberry ice '2767), in which are incrusted a circle of fine peaches, *poached* (249) n vanilla.

The whole is then covered with Italian *meringue* (2383) flavored with Maraschino, and laid in such a way that those portions of the peaches which project from the *glaze* remain bare.

Decorate the surface of the omelet with the same *meringue;* sprinkle it with *icing sugar* (2436a), and set it to a *glaze* quickly.

2471—NEAPOLITAN SURPRISE OMELET, also called BOMBE VESUVE
Omelette en Surprise à la Napolitaine ou Bombe Vesuve

Garnish the bed of *Génoise* (2376) with coatings of vanilla and strawberry ice (2766), alternated with layers of broken glacé-chestnut. Cover the whole with Italian *meringue* (2383) prepared with Kirsch. Keep this flat and somewhat thick towards the center. On top, set a *barquette* of a size in proportion to the omelet, made with the pastry-bag with ordinary *meringue* and baked in the oven without browning. Decorate with Italian *meringue,* covering the *barquette* in so doing, and quickly brown the omelet in the oven. When about to serve, garnish the omelet with Jubilee cherries (2566), and light at the last moment.

2472—SURPRISE OMELET ELIZABETH *Omelette en Surprise Elizabeth*

Garnish the bed of *Génoise* with vanilla ice and crystallized-violets.

Cover it with *meringue;* decorate its surface with crystallized-violets, and treat the omelet as in (2466).

When about to serve it, cover the omelet with a veil of spun sugar.

2473—SURPRISE OMELET NERON *Omelette en Surprise Néron*

Make the bed of *Génoise* round instead of oval; set it on a round dish, and fill it with some sort of ice, which should be shaped like a blunt cone. Cover with *meringue;* set a small case on the top, made from *meringue,* as explained under (2471), but round instead of oval; conceal all but its inside with *meringue,* decorating the omelet in so doing, and set to brown quickly.

When about to serve, pour a glass of heated rum into the *meringue* case and light it.

2474—SYLPHS' SURPRISE OMELET *Omelette en Surprise des Sylphes*

Dip a freshly-cooked *savarin* (2371) into a syrup of maraschino, and stick it on a base of dry paste equal in size.

In the center of the *savarin* set a bed of *Génoise* sufficiently thick to reach half-way up the former.

At the last moment, turn out upon this bed an iced strawberry *mousse* (2766), made in an iced *madeleine-mould,* the diameter of which should be that of the opening of the *savarin*. Cover the *mousse* with a coat of Italian *meringue* (2383) with kirsch, shaping it like a cone of which the base rests upon the top of the *savarin*.

With a pastry-bag, fitted with a small tube, quickly decorate the cone, as also the *savarin*, with the same *meringue;* brown it in the oven, and serve it instantly.

2475—VARIOUS SURPRISE OMELETS *Omelettes Diverses en Surprise*

With the general example given this kind of omelet may be indefinitely varied by changing the ice preparation inside.

The superficial appearance remains the same, but every change in the inside filling should be made known in the title of the dish.

PANNEQUETS

2476—PANNEQUETS WITH JAM *Pannequets aux Confitures*

Prepare some very thin pancakes (2403); spread them with some kind of jam, roll them up, trim them at a slant at either end, and cut them into two diamond shapes.

Place these diamonds on a tray, sprinkle them with *icing sugar,* set them to *glaze* in a hot oven, and serve them on a napkin.

2477—CREAM PANNEQUETS *Pannequets à la Crème*

Spread the pancakes (2403) with *frangipan cream* (2399), and sprinkle the latter with crushed macaroons. For the rest of the procedure follow (2476).

2478—MERINGUED PANNEQUETS *Pannequets Meringuées*

Spread the pancakes (2403) with Italian *meringue* (2383), flavored with kirsch and maraschino; roll them up, cut them into diamond shapes as above, and set them on a tray. Decorate them by means of the pastry-bag with the same *meringue;* sprinkle them with *icing sugar,* and set them to brown quickly in the oven.

2479—PUDDINGS *Puddings*

American and English puddings are almost innumerable; but many of them lie more within the pastrycook's than the cook's province, and their enumeration here could not serve a very useful purpose. The name Pudding is, moreover, applied to a whole host of preparations which are really nothing more than custards—as, for example, "custard pudding." If both of the foregoing kinds of puddings be passed over, puddings proper, which belong to hot sweets may be divided into eight classes, of which I shall first give the general recipes, from which all pudding desserts given hereafter are derived. The six classes are:—

(1) Puddings with cream.
(2) Fruit puddings.
(3) Plum puddings.
(4) Bread puddings.
(5) Rice and paste puddings.
(6) Soufflé puddings.

Puddings permit various accompanying sauces, which will be given in each recipe. The majority of puddings may be accompanied by stewed fruit, Melba sauce, or whipped cream "à la Chantilly."

PUDDINGS WITH CREAM

2480—ALMOND PUDDING   *Pudding aux Amandes*

Make a preparation for *soufflé pudding* (2505), moistened with *almond milk* (2506). Pour it into well-buttered moulds, sprinkled inside with slivered and grilled almonds (2338).

Set to *poach* in the *bain-marie* (water-bath). As an accompaniment serve a *sabayon* (2408) prepared with white wine and flavored with *orgeat*.

2481—ENGLISH ALMOND PUDDING *Pudding aux Amandes à l'Anglaise*

Mix to the consistency of a cream four oz. of butter and five oz. of powdered sugar; add eight oz. of finely-chopped almonds, a pinch of salt, a half tablespoon of orange-flower water, two eggs, two egg-yolks, and one-sixth pint of cream. Pour this preparation into a buttered deep pie-dish or casserole, and cook in a *bain-marie* (water-bath) in the oven.

N.B.—English puddings of any kind are served in the dishes or bowls in which they have cooked.

2482—SPONGE CAKE PUDDING   *Pudding de Bisquit*

Crush eight oz. of sponge ladyfingers in a saucepan, and moisten them with one pint of boiling milk containing five oz. of sugar. Stir the whole over the fire, and add five oz. of candied fruit, cut into dice and mixed with currants (both ingredients having been steeped in kirsch), three egg-yolks, four oz. of melted butter, and the whites of five eggs beaten to a stiff froth.

Set to *poach* in a *bain-marie* (water-bath) in a low, even *Charlotte*

mould, or in a deep pie-dish or casserole, and serve an apricot sauce
(2410) at the same time.

2483—CABINET PUDDING   *Pudding de Cabinet*

Garnish a buttered *cylinder-mould* with sponge ladyfingers or
slices of buttered biscuit, saturated with some kind of liqueur,
arranging them in alternate layers with a *salpicon* of candied fruit
and currants, soaked in liqueur. Here and there spread a little
apricot jam.

Fill up the mould, little by little, with preparation (2639), flavored
according to taste. *Poach* in a *bain-marie* (water-bath).

Turn out the pudding at the last moment, and coat it with
English custard flavored with vanilla.

2484—FRUIT PUDDING   *Pudding de Fruits*

This pudding requires very careful treatment. The custard (2639)
which serves as its base is the same as that of Cabinet Pudding, except that it is thickened by seven eggs and seven egg-yolks per quart
of milk. This preparation is, moreover, combined with a *purée* of
fruit suited to the pudding.

Procedure: Butter a mould; set it in a *bain-marie* (water-bath),
and pour a few tablespoons of the custard into it. Let it set, and
upon this set custard sprinkle a layer of suitable fruit, sliced. This
fruit may be apricots, peaches, pears, etc. Cover the fruit with a
fresh coat of custard, but more copiously than in the first case; let
this custard set as before; cover it with fruit, and proceed in the
same order until the mould is full.

It is, in short, another form of aspic-jelly preparation, but hot
instead of cold. If the solidification of the layers of custard were
not ensured, the fruit would fall to the bottom of the mould instead
of remaining distributed between the layers of custard, and the
result would be the collapse of the pudding as soon as it was turned
out.

Continue the cooking in the *bain-marie* (water-bath); let the
preparation stand a few minutes before turning it out, and serve at
the same time a sauce made from the same fruit as that used for
the pudding.

2485—APPLE PUDDING   *Pudding aux Pommes*

Prepare a suet paste from one lb. of flour, ten oz. of finely-chopped
beef suet, quarter of a pint of water and a pinch of salt.

Let the paste rest for an hour, and roll it out to a thickness of one-third of an inch.

With this layer of paste, line a well-buttered *dome-mould* or large pudding-bowl. Garnish with sliced apples mixed with powdered sugar and flavored with a chopped piece of lemon peel.

Close the mould with a well-sealed-down layer of paste; wrap the mould in a piece of linen, which should be firmly tied with string; plunge it into a saucepan containing boiling water, and in the case of a quart pudding-bowl or mould, let it cook for about three hours.

N.B.—This pudding may be made with other fleshy fruit, as also with certain vegetables such as the pumpkin, etc.

2486—PLUM PUDDING   *Plum Pudding*

Put into a bowl one lb. of chopped beef suet; one lb. of crumbed bread slices; half lb. of flour; half lb. of peeled and chopped apples; half lb. each of Malaga raisins, currants and sultana raisins; two oz. each of candied orange, lemon and citron peel, cut into small dice; two oz. of ginger; four oz. of chopped almonds; eight oz. of powdered sugar; the juice and the chopped rind of half an orange and half a lemon; one-third oz. of mixed spices, containing a large quantity of cinnamon; three eggs; quarter of a pint of rum or brandy, and one-third of a pint of stout. The fruit should, if possible, have previously steeped in liqueur for a long time.

Mix the whole thoroughly.

Pour the preparation into white earthenware pudding-bowls, with projecting rims; press it into them, and then wrap them in a buttered and flour-dusted cloth or dampened vegetable parchment which tie into a knot on top.

Cook in boiling water or in steam for four hours.

When about to serve, sprinkle the puddings with heated brandy or rum, and light them, or accompany them, either with a *sabayon* (2408) with rum, with Brandy Butter (as directed under "Gil-Blas pancakes" (2445) but without sugar), or with an English custard thickened with arrowroot or cornstarch.

2487—AMERICAN PUDDING   *Pudding à l'Américaine*

Put into a bowl two and a half oz. of soft bread-crumbs; three oz. of powdered sugar; three oz. of flour; two and a half oz. of marrow and an equal quantity of beef suet (both chopped); three oz. of candied fruit cut into dice; one egg and three egg-yolks, a pinch of grated orange or lemon rind; a little nutmeg and cinnamon, and a liqueur-glass of brandy or rum.

Mix the whole; pour the preparation into a buttered and floured mould or bowl, and cook in the *bain-marie* (water-bath).

Serve a *sabayon* (2408) with rum at the same time.

2488—MARROW PUDDING   *Pudding   a Moëlle*

Melt half a lb. of beef-marrow and two oz. of beef suet, in a double-boiler, and let it get tepid. Then work this fat in a bowl with half a lb. of powdered sugar; three oz. of bread-crumbs, dipped in milk and pressed; three whole eggs and eight egg-yolks; half a lb. of candied fruit, cut into dice; three oz. of sultana raisins and two oz. of seeded, Malaga raisins.

Pour this preparation into an even, deep, buttered and floured border-mould; and *poach* in the *bain-marie* (water-bath).

Serve a *sabayon* (2408) with rum at the same time.

BREAD PUDDINGS

2489—ENGLISH BREAD PUDDING   *Pudding au Pain à l'Anglaise*

Butter some thin slices of bread and distribute over them some currants and sultana raisins, plumped in tepid water and well drained. Set these slices in a deep pie-dish or casserole; cover with preparation (2638), and *poach* in the oven.

2490—FRENCH BREAD PUDDING   *Pudding au Pain à la Française*

Soak two-thirds of a lb. of soft white bread-crumb in one and three-quarter pints of boiled milk, flavored with vanilla and containing eight oz. of sugar. Rub through a sieve and add: four whole eggs, six egg-yolks, and four egg-whites, beaten stiff.

Pour this preparation into a deep, buttered *border-mould,* dusted with bread-crumbs; and *poach* in *bain-marie* (water-bath).

As an accompaniment, serve either an English custard, a vanilla-flavored *sabayon,* or a fruit sauce.

2491—GERMAN BREAD PUDDING   *Pudding au Pain Allemand*

Soak two-thirds of a lb. of soft brown bread-crumbs (whole rye, etc.), in one and three-quarter pints of Rhine wine, Moselle or beer, containing half a lb. of brown sugar and a little cinnamon. Rub through a sieve and add four eggs, six egg-yolks, five oz. of melted butter, and the whites of four eggs beaten stiff. *Poach* in a *bain-marie* (water-bath) as in the preceding case. The accompaniment to this pudding is invariably a fruit syrup.

2492—SCOTCH BREAD PUDDING   *Pudding au Pain d'Ecossaise*

Proceed exactly as for (2490), but add five oz. of sliced seasonable fruit. Mould and *poach* in the same way, and serve a red-currant sauce flavored with raspberries, as an accompaniment.

PASTE PUDDINGS

2493—TAPIOCA PUDDING   *Pudding au Tapioca*

Sprinkle eight oz. of tapioca into one and three-quarter pints of boiling milk, containing four oz. of sugar, a pinch of salt and three oz. of butter.

Cook in the oven for twenty minutes; transfer the preparation to another saucepan, and add to it six egg-yolks, two and a half oz. of butter, and the whites of four eggs beaten to a stiff froth.

Pour the whole into a well-buttered *cylinder-mould*, sprinkled with tapioca, and *poach* in the *bain-marie* (water-bath) until the preparation seems springy to the touch. Let the pudding stand for seven or eight minutes before turning it out. Serve an English custard, a *sabayon* or a fruit sauce as accompaniment.

2494—SAGO PUDDING   *Pudding au Sagon*

Proceed as above, but substitute sago for the tapioca, and sprinkle the inside of the mould with sago. The treatment and accompaniments are the same.

2495—SEMOLINA PUDDING   *Pudding à la Semoule*

Proceed as for (2493), but use semolina instead of tapioca, and sprinkle the mould with granulated semolina (fine farina).

2496—VERMICELLI PUDDING   *Pudding à Vermicelle*

Proceed as for (2493), but use vermicelli, and sprinkle the mould with bits of vermicelli, which should not be broken up too much.

2497—FRESH MADE NOODLE PUDDING

Pudding aux Nouilles Fraiches

Proceed in exactly the same way as for (2493).

2498—ENGLISH TAPIOCA, SAGO, AND SEMOLINA PUDDINGS

Puddings de Tapioca, Sagon, et Semoule à l'Anglaise

Whatever be the ingredient used, it should be cooked in very slightly-sugared milk, flavored according to fancy, and in the quantities given above. Thicken with two eggs per pint of the preparation; pour the whole into a buttered pie-dish or casserole, and cook in the oven in a *bain-marie* (water-bath).

N.B.—All English puddings of this class are made in the same way, and, as already stated, are served in the dish in which they have cooked.

2499—BRAZILIAN PUDDING *Pudding Brésilien*

Make the preparation for tapioca pudding and pour it into a mould, coated with sugar cooked to the *caramel* stage (360° F.).

Poach in a *bain-marie* (water-bath) and serve plain.

2500—CHEVREUSE PUDDING *Pudding à la Chevreuse*

This is semolina pudding served with a Sabayon (2408), flavored with kirsch.

2501—RICE PUDDING *Pudding au Riz*

Prepare the rice as directed under (2404), and mix with it (per lb. of raw rice) the whites of fifteen eggs beaten to a stiff froth. Mould in buttered moulds sprinkled with *raspings*.

The cooking and the accompaniments are the same as for (2493, 2494), etc.

2502—ENGLISH RICE PUDDING *Pudding au Riz à l'Anglaise*

The quantities for this pudding are: six oz. of rice, one quart of milk (flavored according to taste), two oz. of sugar and three oz. of butter. The grains of rice should be kept somewhat firm, but the whole should be rather liquid. Thicken with three eggs; cook the preparation in the oven, in a pie-dish or casserole; and on taking the pudding out of the oven sprinkle its surface with *icing sugar*.

2503—RICE AND CHOCOLATE PUDDING *Pudding de Riz au Chocolat*

Add two oz. of chocolate to every lb. of the preparation of rice, made after (2404), and combine with the whites of three eggs beaten to a fairly stiff froth; pour the preparation into a buttered pie-dish or casserole, and cook in the oven.

Serve some chocolate custard (combined with its bulk of whipped cream) separately.

N.B.—This sweet may be served hot or cold.

SOUFFLÉD PUDDINGS

2504—SAXON PUDDING *Pudding Saxon*

Work four oz. of butter to a cream in a bowl. Add four oz. of powdered sugar and four oz. of sifted flour, and dilute with two-thirds pint of boiled milk.

Boil this preparation, stirring it the while; and dry it over a hot fire as in the case of a *panada* for a "Pâte à choux" (2374).

Take off the fire; thicken with five egg-yolks; and then carefully mix with it the five whites beaten to a stiff froth. Pour into well-buttered moulds, and *poach* in a *bain-marie* (water-bath).

As an accompaniment serve an English custard or a Sabayon, flavored according to fancy.

2505—ALMOND SOUFFLE PUDDING *Pudding Soufflé aux Amandes*

Make a preparation as for (2504), but use almond milk (2506) instead of cow's milk. Pour the preparation into buttered moulds, sprinkled with slivered and grilled almonds, and *poach* in a *bain-marie* (water-bath).

As an accompaniment serve a white-wine Sabayon (2408) flavored with *orgeat*.

2506—SOUFFLE PUDDING DENISE ALMOND MILK
Pudding Soufflé Denise au Lait d'Amandes

Finely pound four oz. of freshly-washed and peeled almonds, and add, from time to time, a few drops of fresh water. When the almonds form a smooth paste, add the necessary quantity of water to them to produce one pint of milk. Strain through muslin and slightly twist the latter in order to squeeze out all the liquid.

With this almond milk, dilute three oz. of flour and three oz. of rice cream, mixed in a saucepan, and take care that no lumps form. Strain the whole through a sieve, and add five oz. of sugar, three oz. of butter and a little salt.

Set the saucepan on the stove; boil, stirring the while, and then stir briskly with a spatula until the preparation acquires the consistency of a thick paste and falls from the spatula without leaving any portions sticking. Pour this paste into a bowl and combine with: first, little by little, two oz. of fresh butter; then, eight egg-yolks, two ounces of finely-pounded almonds moistened with a tablespoon of kirsch and as much maraschino, and the whites of five eggs beaten to a stiff froth.

This pudding is cooked in a *bain-marie* (water-bath) in one of the following ways:

In a buttered deep pie-dish. In this case, on taking the pudding out of the *bain-marie,* sprinkle its surface with icing sugar, and criss-cross it with a red-hot iron.

Or in a shallow, buttered and flour dredged, *Charlotte-mould.*

Or in fairly shallow, buttered *dome-moulds,* lined inside with slices one inch in diameter, stamped (by means of a fancy-cutter) out of a layer of *Génoise* or a layer of sponge cake preparation, about one-third of an inch thick.

In the two last cases, the pudding is coated with an apricot sauce (2410), mixed with the almond milk, and a sauceboat of the same sauce is served separately.

2507—LEMON SOUFFLE PUDDING   *Pudding Soufflé au Citron*

Make the preparation for (2504), and flavor it with a piece of lemon rind. The treatment is the same.

Serve an English custard (2397), flavored with lemon separately.

2508—ORANGE, CURACAO, ANISETTE, AND BENEDICTINE PUDDINGS   *Puddings Soufflés à l'Orange, au Curaçao, à l'Anisette, et à la Benedictine*

For all these puddings the procedure is the same as for (2504), and only the flavor changes.

Accompany each with an English custard (2397), flavored like the particular pudding.

2509—INDIAN SOUFFLE PUDDING   *Pudding Soufflé à l'Indienne*

Take some soufflé-pudding preparation and add to it two oz. of powdered ginger, and five oz. of candied ginger, cut in small dice. Proceed in the same way as for (2504).

As an accompaniment, serve an English custard (2397) flavored with ginger.

2510—CHESTNUT SOUFFLE PUDDING   *Pudding Soufflé aux Marrons*

Cook two lbs. of peeled chestnuts in a light, vanilla-flavored syrup.

Rub them through a sieve, add five oz. of powdered sugar and three oz. of butter to the *purée,* and dry it over a hot fire. Thicken it with eight egg-yolks and finish it with the whites of six eggs, beaten to a stiff froth.

Poach in buttered moulds in a *bain-marie* (water-bath).

As an accompaniment, serve, either an English custard (2397), or a vanilla-flavored apricot syrup (2410).

2511—MOUSSELINE PUDDING   *Pudding Mousseline*

Work four oz. of butter and four oz. of powdered sugar to a cream, and add the yolks of ten eggs, one by one; meanwhile stirring the preparation.

Set the latter on a moderate fire until it coats the withdrawn spoon; then immediately add the whites of seven eggs beaten to a stiff froth.

Pour the whole into a deep, buttered *border-mould,* which only half fill, in view of the expansion of the preparation while cooking.

Poach in a *bain-marie* (water-bath) for about thirty minutes, and let the pudding stand for ten minutes before turning it out.

As an accompaniment serve a light Sabayon (2408) or a fruit sauce.

2512—REGENCE SOUFFLE PUDDING   *Pudding Soufflé Régence*

Make a *soufflé*-pudding preparation flavored with vanilla, and *poach* it in a *bain-marie* (water-bath), in a mould coated with sugar cooked to the *caramel* stage (360° F.). Serve an English custard (2397), prepared with caramel, separately.

2513—SOUFFLE PUDDING A LA REINE   *Pudding Soufflé à la Reine*

Take some vanilla-flavored, *soufflé*-pudding preparation. Take a mould with a central tube; butter it, and sprinkle it with chopped pistachios and crushed macaroons. Set the preparation in the mould in layers, alternated by coats of chopped pistachios and crushed macaroons; and *poach* in a *bain-marie* (water-bath).

As an accompaniment serve an English custard (2397) combined with *pralin.*

2514—SOUFFLE PUDDING A LA ROYALE   *Pudding Soufflé à la Royale*

Line the bottom and sides of a buttered *Charlotte-mould* with thin slices of sponge cake spread with jam and rolled up. Fill the mould with a *soufflé*-pudding preparation, and *poach* in a *bain-marie* (water-bath).

Serve an apricot sauce (2410) flavored with Marsala, separately.

2515—SOUFFLE PUDDING SANS-SOUCI   *Pudding Soufflé Sans-Souci*

Copiously butter a mould, and sprinkle its bottom and sides with well-washed and drained currants. Fill with a *soufflé*-pudding preparation, combined per two lbs. with one lb. of peeled apples, cut in dice and cooked in butter.

Poach in a *bain-marie* (water-bath).

2516—SOUFFLE PUDDING VESUVIENNE   *Pudding Soufflé Vésuvienne*

Make a *soufflé*-pudding preparation, and add to it for the quantities given in the original recipe one and a half oz. of tomato jam and the same quantity of seeded Malaga raisins. *Poach* in a *bain-marie* (water-bath) in a mould with a central tube.

When the pudding is turned out, surround it with apricot sauce (2410), and pour in the middle some heated rum, and light when serving.

2517—ROLY-POLY PUDDING   *Rolly Pudding*

Proceed as for (2361): prepare a firm paste from one lb. of flour, nine oz. of chopped suet, one and a half oz. of sugar, a pinch of salt, and one-sixth pint of water. Let this paste rest for one hour before using it.

Roll it out to the shape of a rectangle one-fifth of an inch thick; spread a layer of jam upon it, and roll it up like a jelly roll.

Wrap it in a buttered and flour dredged cloth or vegetable parchment, and cook it in boiling water or in steam for one and a half hours.

When about to serve, cut the roll into slices half an inch thick, and arrange them in a crown. As an accompaniment serve a fruit sauce.

2518—RISSOLES   *Rissoles*

The preparation of *rissoles* for desserts is the same as that for *rissoles* served as hors-d'œuvres, except that the former are garnished with marmalade or jam, with a fruit *salpicon* or with stewed fruit, with plain or *pralined* creams, etc.

The best paste for the purpose is derived from puff-paste (2366) trimmings.

The shape of *rissoles* varies very much. They may be shaped like half-moons, turnovers, small, round or oval patties, etc.

Rissoles for desserts are also frequently made from ordinary *brioche* paste (2368), and constitute a variety of Viennese fritters. In this case they are invariably mentioned on the menu as "à la Dauphine."

2519—SOUFFLES
Soufflés

Although *soufflés* are generally served unaccompanied, some stewed, seasonable fruit, or a *macédoine* of fresh fruit, may, nevertheless, be served with them. This, of course, only applies to *soufflés* with a fruit base.

I have already given the recipes for *soufflés* (2405); I need now, therefore, only give the peculiarities of each particular *soufflé*.

2520—FRUIT SOUFFLE IN A CROUSTADE
Soufflé de Fruits en Croustade

Line a round, shallow, well-buttered, *croustade-mould* with a very thin layer of sweetened paste. Spread some vanilla-flavored, stewed apples on the bottom, and upon it lay a filling of various seasonable fresh stewed fruits—quartered if large. The mould ought now to be half-filled.

Fill it up with a vanilla-flavored *soufflé* preparation, and cook it in a moderate oven for about twenty-five minutes.

On taking it from the oven, carefully turn it out on a dish; pour a few tablespoons of heated rum into it, and light it when serving.

2521—ALMOND SOUFFLE
Soufflé aux Amandes

Make a preparation of *soufflé* with cream, but use almond milk (2506) instead of cow's milk, add one and a half oz. of slightly-grilled, chopped almonds, per half pint of almond milk. Put in a dish and cook in the usual way.

2522—SOUFFLE WITH FRESH ALMONDS
Soufflé aux Amandes Fraîches

Proceed exactly as above, but use fresh slivered almonds instead of grilled, chopped ones.

2523—SOUFFLE WITH FILBERT
Soufflé aux Avelines

Make the *soufflé* preparation from milk in which two oz. of filbert *pralin* per one-sixth pint have previously been steeped.

Put on a dish and cook the *soufflé* in the usual way.

2524—CAMARGO SOUFFLE
Soufflé Camargo

Make a *soufflé* preparation of tangerines, and another of filberts as above. Put the two preparations in layers, alternated by ladyfingers, saturated with Curaçao liqueur.

2525—PAULETTE SOUFFLE   *Soufflé Paulette*

Take vanilla-flavored *soufflé* preparation, thickened somewhat more than the ordinary kind, and add to it five tablespoons of strawberry *purée*. Serve some well-cooled strawberries, coated with raspberry *purée,* separately.

2526—CHERRY SOUFFLE   *Soufflé aux Cerises*

Prepare a *soufflé* with Kirsch, accompany it with some stewed pitted cherries, covered with a raspberry *purée.*

2527—STRAWBERRY SOUFFLE   *Soufflé aux Fraises*

This is a *soufflé* with Kirsch, accompanied by iced strawberries steeped in orange juice.

2528—ORIENTALE POMEGRANATE SOUFFLE

Soufflé aux Grenades à l'Orientale

Make a *soufflé* preparation, slightly flavored with vanilla. Arrange it in layers in a *timbale,* alternated by sponge ladyfingers saturated with Grenadine and Kirsch. On taking the *soufflé* from the oven, cover it with a veil of spun sugar, and sprinkle the *soufflé* with small candies, flavored with Grenadine, in imitation of pomegranate seeds.

2529—JAVA SOUFFLE   *Soufflé Javanais*

Make the *soufflé* preparation, but use tea instead of milk, and add one and a half oz. of chopped pistachios per one-sixth pint of the tea.

2530—CHARTREUSE SOUFFLE   *Soufflé Lérina*

Take some ordinary *soufflé* preparation, flavored with Lérina liqueur, which is a kind of Chartreuse, made in the Lérins islands.

2531—SOUFFLE WITH LIQUEUR   *Soufflé aux Liqueurs*

This *soufflé* may be made, either from the *soufflé* with cream preparation or from that with fruit, given in the note.

The *soufflés* made from cream are flavored with such liqueurs as rum, curaçao, anisette, vanilla, etc.

Those made from fruit are flavored with Kirsch, Kümmel, etc.

2532—LUCULLUS SOUFFLE   *Soufflé Lucullus*

Set a *savarin* (2371), saturated with kirsch-flavored syrup, upon a dish, and surround it with a band of paper, tied on with string, in order to prevent the *soufflé* from drying during the cooking process.

Make a *soufflé* preparation with a fruit base, set it in the center of the *savarin,* and cook it in the usual way.

2533—HILDA SOUFFLE
Soufflé Hilda

This is a lemon *soufflé,* accompanied by fine strawberries, well chilled and coated with a *purée* of fresh raspberries.

2534—ORLEANS SOUFFLE
Soufflé à l'Orléans

Take some cream *soufflé*-preparation, combined with pieces of Jeanne-d'Arc biscuits (kind of small sponge cakes), saturated with peach liqueur and kirsch, and one oz. each of half-sugared cherries and angelica, cut into dice.

2535—PALMYRA SOUFFLE
Soufflé Palmyre

Take some vanilla-flavored *soufflé* preparation. Set it in a *timbale,* in layers alternated by sponge ladyfingers saturated with anisette and Kirsch. Cook in the usual way.

2536—PRALINE SOUFFLE
Soufflé Praliné

Take some vanilla-flavored *soufflé* preparation; add to it two ounces of almond *pralin* which should have previously steeped in milk. When the *soufflé* is ready, sprinkle its surface with grilled chopped almonds or crushed, burnt almonds.

2537—ROTHSCHILD SOUFFLE
Soufflé Rothschild

Take some cream *soufflé*-preparation, combined with three ounces of candied fruit, cut into dice and steeped in Dantzig Gold Wasser, a brandy, containing plenty of gold leaf spangles.

When the *soufflé* is almost cooked, set on it a border of fine strawberries (in season), or half-sugared, preserved cherries.

It should be remembered, however, that the correct procedure demands the use of strawberries in full season.

2538—ROYALE SOUFFLE
Soufflé à la Royale

Take some vanilla-flavored *soufflé*-preparation. Put it in a *timbale* in alternate layers with sponge ladyfingers, saturated with Kirsch; and distribute over it such fruits as pineapple, cherries, angelica and grapes—all cut into dice, and previously steeped in Kirsch.

2539—VANILLA SOUFFLE
Soufflé à la Vanille

Take some cream *soufflé*-preparation, made from milk in which a stick of vanilla has been previously steeped or cooked.

2540—VIOLET SOUFFLE　　　　　　　*Soufflé aux Violets*

Take some vanilla-flavored *soufflé* preparation, combined with crushed crystallized violets. When the *soufflé* is ready, set on it a crown of large crystallized violets, and cook in the usual way.

2541—SUBRICS　　　　　　　　　　　　　　*Subrics*

Into one pint of vanilla-flavored boiled milk, containing three and a half oz. of sugar, drop four oz. of semolina. Add one and a half oz. of butter and a few grains of salt; mix thoroughly, and gently cook in the oven under cover for twenty-five minutes.

Thicken with six egg-yolks, and spread the preparation in layers two-thirds of an inch thick on a buttered pan. Pass a piece of butter over the surface to prevent its drying, and leave to cool.

Then cut out this preparation into rounds three inches in diameter.

Heat some clarified butter (175) in a frying-pan; set the rounds in it; brown them on both sides, and arrange them in a circle. Garnish the center of each round with a tablespoon of red-currant jelly, or very firm quince jelly.

TIMBALES

2542—D'AREMBERG TIMBALE　　　　*Timbale d'Aremberg*

Line a buttered *Charlotte-mould* with some fairly firm Brioche paste (2368). Fill the mould with quartered pears, cooked in vanilla-flavored syrup, kept rather firm and alternated by apricot jam.

Close the *timbale* with a layer of the same paste, well sealed down round the slightly-moistened edges, and cut a slit in the middle for the escape of steam. Cook in a good moderate oven for about forty minutes.

On taking the *timbale* out of the oven, turn it out on a dish, and accompany it with a maraschino-flavored apricot sauce (2410).

2543—BOURDALOUE TIMBALE　　　　*Timbale Bourdaloue*

Prepare a dry paste (2362), combined with four ounces of finely-chopped almonds per one lb. of flour.

With this paste line a buttered *timbale* mould, and garnish it with various stewed fruits, alternated by layers of *frangipan* cream (2399). Cover with a layer of the same paste, and bake in a good moderate oven.

When the *timbale* is turned out, coat it with a vanilla-flavored apricot syrup.

2544—MARIE-LOUISE TIMBALE   *Timbale Marie-Louise*

Take a stale *Génoise* baked in a deep *Charlotte-mould;* press the blade of a knife into it and cut it all round, leaving a base.

Remove the inside in one piece which should resemble a large cork in shape. Cut this piece into slices half-inch thick; coat each slice with Italian *meringue* (2383), and, upon the latter, spread a *salpicon* of peaches, cherries and pineapple.

Coat the outside of the *timbale* with the same *meringue,* and decorate it; put the slices back inside, and set them one upon the other. Owing to the inserted filling these slices naturally project above the sides of the *timbale;* surround them with a border of *poached* peaches, separated by a bit of *meringue.*

Put the *timbale* in a mild oven to brown the *meringue,* and serve a Kirsch-flavored peach sauce (2368) at the same time.

2545—MONTMORENCY TIMBALE   *Timbale Montmorency*

Bake a brioche in a mould of the required size. When it is quite cold, remove all the soft crumb from its inside, leaving a thickness of three-quarters of an inch on the bottom and sides. Coat all round, by means of a brush, with apricot jam cooked to the *small-thread* stage (215° F.), and decorate with pieces of puff-paste in the shape of crescents, diamonds, circles, etc., baked without browning in a moderate oven. When about to serve, pour in a filling of pitted cherries, cooked in a thin syrup, thickened with raspberry-flavored red-currant jelly.

2546—PARISIENNE TIMBALE   *Timbale à la Parisienne*

Bake a brioche in a *Charlotte-mould,* and, when it is quite cold, remove the crumb from its inside as above. Coat the outside with apricot jam, and decorate with candied fruit. When about to serve, pour into it a filling consisting of peeled and quartered pears, apples, peaches and apricots, cooked in vanilla-flavored syrup; pineapple cut into large dice, diamond shapes of angelica; half-almonds; and raisins, plumped in tepid water. Mix this filling with a Kirsch-flavored apricot *purée* (2410).

2547—FAVART TIMBALE   *Timbale à la Favart*

Bake a brioche in a *Richelieu-mould,* and hollow it out and decorate it as above. The filling of this *timbale* consists of only whole or halved fruit, and vanilla-flavored chestnuts; and these are mixed with Kirsch-flavored apricot syrup (2410), combined with one quart of a *purée* of chestnut pieces.

Pour the filling into the *timbale* just before serving.

Hot Fruit Entremets

2548—APRICOTS   *Abricots*
Whether fresh or preserved, apricots used for desserts should
always be peeled. When preserved apricots are used, it is well to
cook them again before using them, for sometimes they are inclined
to be too firm.

2549—BOURDALOUE APRICOTS   *Abricots Bourdaloue*
Prepare a flawn-crust for custards, and bake it without browning.
Fill its bottom with a layer of thin *frangipan* cream (2399), combined with crushed macaroons. Upon this cream set some half-
apricots, *poached* in vanilla-flavored syrup, and cover them with a
layer of the same cream.

Sprinkle the surface with crushed macaroons and melted butter
and *glaze* quickly.

N.B.—The above is the usual procedure, but fruit "à la Bourdaloue" may also be prepared in the following ways: Set the fruit in a
shallow *timbale* between two layers of cream, the upper one of
which should be covered with *gratin;* or set the fruit in a border of
rice or semolina, with the same coat of *gratin* upon the cream; or
set the fruit in a border of *Génoise,* combined with apricots.

2550—COLBERT APRICOTS   *Abricots Colbert*
Poach some fine half-apricots in syrup, keeping them somewhat
firm.

Drain them; dry them, and fill their hollows with "rice for desserts" (2404) in such a way as to reconstruct the fruit. Treat them
à l'Anglaise, with very fine bread-crumbs; fry just before serving,
and drain. Stick a small piece of angelica into each apricot, in
imitation of the stems, and set them on a napkin.

Serve a Kirsch-flavored apricot sauce (2410) separately.

2551—CONDE APRICOTS   *Abricots Condé*
On a round dish prepare a border of vanilla-flavored, sweet rice,
either by means of a knife, or by means of an even, buttered, *ring-
mould.*

Upon this ring set some apricots *poached* in syrup; decorate with
candied fruit, and coat with a Kirsch-flavored apricot syrup (2410).

2552—CONDE APRICOTS (2nd METHOD) *Abricots Condé*

Set a crown of small *Génoise* round slices on a dish; on each round slice set a fine *poached* half-apricot face up, and set a half-sugared cherry in the hollow of each half-apricot. In the middle of the crown arrange a pyramid of rice croquettes, the size and shape of apricots.

Serve a Kirsch-flavored apricot sauce (2410) separately.

2553—CUSSY APRICOTS *Abricots Cussy*

Garnish the flat side of some macaroons with a layer of smooth fruit *salpicon,* mixed with an apricot *purée;* set a fine *poached* half-apricot on each macaroon, coat with Italian *meringue* (2383); arrange in the form of a crown, and place the dish in a moderate oven for a few minutes to dry, but not to brown, the *meringue.*

Serve a Kirsch-flavored apricot sauce separately.

2554—APRICOTS GRATIN *Abricots Gratinés*

Spread an even layer, one inch thick, of stiff stewed apples or stewed semolina (prepared like rice for desserts) (2404) on a dish. Set on some fine half-apricots *poached* in syrup; entirely cover the latter with a somewhat thin preparation of *"Pralin* à Condé," sprinkle with icing sugar, and set the dish in the oven to slightly brown the *pralin.*

2555—MERINGUED APRICOTS *Abricots Meringués*

Spread a layer of vanilla-flavored sweet rice on a dish, and set some *poached* half-apricots on it. Cover with ordinary *meringue;* shaping the latter like a dome or a *Charlotte* (2404); decorate with the same *meringue;* sprinkle with icing sugar, and place the dish in the oven in order to slightly cook the *meringue.*

On taking the dish from the oven, garnish the decorative portions alternately with apricot and red-currant jam.

2556—MERINGUED APRICOTS (2nd METHOD) *Abricots Meringués*

Prepare an unbrowned-baked deep crust for custard. Fill the bottom either with a layer of *frangipan* cream or with vanilla-flavored semolina, or sweet rice. Set on this some *poached* half-apricots; cover with *meringue,* smooth the latter on top and all round with the blade of a knife, and decorate with *meringue* by means of a pastry-bag fitted with a small even tube. For the rest of the procedure follow the preceding recipe.

2557—SULTANA APRICOTS   *Abricots Sultane*

Prepare a *Génoise*, cooked in a somewhat deep *border-mould*, and stick it by means of some apricot, cooked to the *small-thread* stage (215° F.), to a base of dry paste (2362) of the same size. Coat it all round with ordinary *meringue*; decorate it with a pastry-bag fitted with a small even tube, and brown it in a moderate oven.

Then fill the inside of the border with a preparation of vanilla-flavored rice, combined with a little *frangipan* cream and some slivered pistachios; taking care to keep the preparation sufficiently stiff to be able to shape it like a dome. Upon the rice set some fine half-apricots, *poached* in vanilla-flavored syrup, and sprinkle these with chopped pistachios.

As an accompaniment serve a syrup prepared with almond milk (2506), and finished with a piece of butter as big as a hazel-nut.

PINEAPPLE (ANANAS)

2558—PINEAPPLE FAVORITE   *Ananas Favorite*

See (2429).

2559—CONDE PINEAPPLE   *Ananas Condé*

Steep in sugar and Kirsch some half-slices of pineapple. Arrange them in a circle upon a border of rice, prepared as directed under (2551); decorate with half-sugared cherries and diamond shapes of angelica, and coat with a Kirsch-flavored apricot syrup (2410).

2560—CREOLE PINEAPPLE   *Ananas à la Créole*

Cook a pineapple in a Kirsch-flavored syrup; cut it lengthwise in two, and cut each half into thin and regular slices.

Line a *dome-mould* with these half-slices, and fill it up with vanilla-flavored rice; leaving a hollow in the middle. Fill this hollow with the pineapple left overs, cut into dice, and custard apples and bananas, likewise cut into dice and cooked in syrup.

Turn out upon a round dish; decorate the top with large leaves of angelica, and surround the base with bananas *poached* in Kirsch-flavored syrup.

Serve a Kirsch-flavored apricot syrup (2410) separately.

BANANAS (BANANES)

2561—BOURDALOUE BANANAS   *Bananes Bourdaloue*

Peel the bananas and *poach* them gently in a vanilla-flavored syrup. For the rest of the operation, proceed as directed under (2549).

2562—CONDE BANANAS   *Bananes Condé*

Poach the bananas in vanilla-flavored syrup, and then treat them as directed under (2551).

2563—MERINGUED BANANAS   *Bananes Meringuées*

Poach the bananas in vanilla-flavored syrup, and then treat them as directed under the apricot recipes (2555 and 2556); leaving them either whole or cutting them into round slices.

2564—BANANAS A LA NORVEGIENNE   *Bananes à la Norvègienne*

Cut a slice of the peel from each banana, and remove the pulp from their insides. Fill the emptied peels, three parts full, with banana ice; and quickly cover the latter with a pastry-bag fitted with a small fancy tube, with an Italian *meringue* (2383) flavored with rum.

Lay the prepared bananas on a dish; set in a pan containing cracked ice, and place the pan in a sufficiently hot oven to ensure the speedy browning of the *meringue*.

2565—SOUFFLE BANANAS   *Bananes Soufflées*

Cut off a quarter of each banana, and remove the pulp from their insides without breaking the peel. Rub this pulp through a sieve; add it to a cream *soufflé*-preparation (2405); finish the latter with the necessary quantity of egg-whites, and fill the emptied peels with it.

Set the filled peels in a star on a dish, and put the latter in the oven for six minutes.

CHERRIES (CERISES)

2566—JUBILEE CHERRIES   *Cerises Jubilée*

Pit some fine cherries; *poach* them in syrup, and set them in small silver *timbales*. Reduce the syrup and thicken it with a little arrowroot or cornstarch, diluted with cold water; allowing one tablespoon of thickening per half-pint of syrup. Cover the cherries with the thickened syrup; pour a teaspoonful of heated Kirsch into each *timbale*, and light each one when serving.

2567—VALERIA CHERRIES   *Cerises Valéria*

Prepare some *tartlet crusts* for sweetened paste. Fill the bottom of each with red-currant ice, combined with cream, and cover the latter with vanilla-flavored, Italian *meringue* (2383), piped on with a pastry-bag. Upon this *meringue* set the pitted cherries, *poached* in sugared Bordeaux wine, and arrange the *tartlets* on a dish.

Lay the dish on a tray containing cracked ice, and set the tray in the oven in order to dry the *meringue*. On taking the dish from the oven, quickly coat the cherries with red-currant syrup; sprinkle the latter with chopped pistachios, and serve the *tartlets* on a napkin.

2568—DEEP CHERRY MERINGUE PIE   *Flan de Cerises Meringue*

Line a buttered spring-form with fine paste: prick the bottom; fill with pitted cherries after the manner of an ordinary pie, and fill up with custard (2397). Cook in the usual way.

On taking the pie out of the oven, remove the rim of the form, and finish the pie like an ordinary *meringue*-one.

N.B.—All fruits used in the preparation of ordinary deep pies may be similarly prepared for *meringue*-coated pies. Only such fruits as strawberries and grapes, which are not cooked with the crust, are unsuited to this kind of preparation.

2569—NECTARINES   *Nectarines ou Brugnons*

Nectarines may be prepared after all the recipes given for peaches. I shall not, therefore, give any recipes which are proper to them. See peaches (2573).

ORANGES AND TANGERINES (ORANGES ET MANDARINES)

2570—ORANGES A LA NORVEGIENNE   *Oranges à la Norvègienne*

Cut a slice of peel from the top of each of the oranges, and scoop out with a spoon. Fill the emptied scooped out skin shells three-parts with orange or tangerine ice, in accordance with the fruit being used, and cover the ice with Italian *meringue* (2383), with a pastry-bag.

Set the dish containing the garnished skin shells on a tray covered with cracked ice, and quickly brown the *meringue* at the *salamander*.

2571—TANGERINES A LA PALIKARE *Mandarines à la Palikare*

Cut the tangerines at the top and remove the sections without breaking the peel. Skin the sections. Fill the peels with rice for desserts (2404), containing a little saffron; mould some of the same rice in a little *dome-mould,* and set it upon a carved bed.

Cover this dome with the tangerine sections; coat the latter with some apricot syrup; and, all round, arrange the rice-garnished peels, opened side down.

2572—SURPRISE ORANGE OR TANGERINE SOUFFLE

Soufflé d'Oranges ou de Mandarines en Surprise

Without splitting them, empty the orange or tangerine peels.

Half-fill them with orange or tangerine ice, according to the fruit being used, and cover the ice with orange- or tangerine-flavored *soufflé*-preparation. Place the dish containing the filled peels upon a tray covered with cracked ice; set in the oven that the *soufflé* may cook quickly, and allow two minutes for tangerines and four minutes for oranges.

PEACHES (PÊCHES)

2573—BOURDALOUE PEACHES *Pêches Bourdaloue*

Poach the peaches (cut into two) in some vanilla-flavored syrup, and then proceed exactly as for (2549).

2574—CONDE PEACHES *Pêches Condé*

Nos. 2551 and 2552 may be applied in every respect to peaches.

2575—CUSSY PEACHES *Pêches Cussy*

Proceed exactly as for (2553).

2576—PEACHES FLAMBEES *Pêches Flambées*

These may be prepared in two ways as follows:—

Poach the peaches whole in a Kirsch-flavored syrup (2418), and set them each in a small *timbale*. Thicken the syrup slightly with arrowroot or cornstarch, and pour it over the peaches. Add some heated Kirsch, and light it when serving.

Or *poach* the peaches as above, and set them on a fresh-strawberry *purée*. Sprinkle the whole with heated Kirsch, and light it at the last moment.

2577—GRATIN PEACHES *Pêches Gratinées*

Proceed exactly as for (2554).

2578—MERINGUED PEACHES   *Pêches Meringuées*

Prepare an unbrowned crust for custard; fill the bottom of it with *frangipan* cream prepared with *pralin,* and upon this cream set whole or halved, *poached* peaches. Cover with *meringue* and finish as explained under (2555).

2579—MAINTENON PEACHES   *Pêches Maintenon*

Take a sponge cake, baked in a dome-mould and completely cooled. Cut it across into slices, and coat each of the latter with *frangipan* cream, combined with a *salpicon* of candied fruit and chopped, grilled almonds.

Join the slices together in such a way as to reconstruct the cake, and cover the latter with Italian *meringue* (2383). Decorate by means of the pastry-bag, and dry in the oven.

Surround the cake with a border of fine half-peaches *poached* in a vanilla-flavored syrup.

2580—VANILLA PEACHES   *Pêches à la Vanille*

Poach the halved or whole peaches in a vanilla-flavored syrup, and set them in a *timbale.* Cover them to within half their height with the syrup used in *poaching,* thickened with arrowroot or cornstarch slightly tinted with pink, and combined with vanilla cream.

PEARS (POIRES)

2581—BOURDALOUE PEARS   *Poires Bourdaloue*

If the pears be of medium size, halve them; if they are large, quarter them. Carefully trim the sections. Cook the pears in a vanilla-flavored syrup, and for the rest of the operation follow (2549).

The remarks appended to (2549) apply equally to pears and to all fruit prepared according to the particular recipe referred to.

2582—CONDE PEARS   *Poires Condé*

Very small pears cut with great care are admirably suited to this dessert. If they are of medium size, halve them. Cook them in vanilla-flavored syrup, and serve them on a border of rice as directed under (2551).

2583—IMPERATRICE PEARS   *Poires à l'Impératrice*

Quarter and properly trim the pears, and cook them in vanilla-flavored syrup. Arrange them in a shallow *timbale* between two layers of vanilla-flavored rice for desserts, combined with a little *frangipan* cream (2399).

Sprinkle the upper layer with crushed macaroons and melted butter, and set the *gratin* to form.

2584—PARISIENNE PEARS *Poires à la Parisienne*

Bake a *Génoise* base in a spring form, and, when it is almost cold, saturate it with Kirsch-flavored syrup.

In the middle of this base set a little dome of vanilla-flavored rice, and surround it with pears, cooked in syrup and set upright. Border them with a ribbon of ordinary *meringue*, squeezed from a pastry-bag, fitted with a fair-sized, fancy tube; by the same means make a fine rosette of *meringue* on top of the dome, and bake this *meringue* in a mild oven.

On taking the dish out of the oven, *glaze* the pears with a brush dipped in rather stiff apricot-syrup, and surround them with a border of half-sugared cherries.

2585—SULTANA PEARS *Poires Sultane*

Halve or quarter the pears; trim them well, and cook them in a vanilla-flavored syrup.

For the rest of the operation follow (2557).

2586—REGENCE PEARS *Poires à la Régence*

Peel the pears; cook them whole in a vanilla-flavored syrup, and let them cool in the syrup. When they are cold cut them in two lengthwise, slightly hollow out the inside of each half; garnish the hollow with rice for desserts, combined with a quarter of its weight of *frangipan* cream and a fine *salpicon* of candied fruit, steeped in Kirsch.

Join the two halves of each pear, and treat them *à l'anglaise* with very fine bread-crumbs.

Fry them at the last moment, and, on taking them out of the fat, stick an angelica stalk as a stem into each. Set them on a napkin, and serve a Kirsch-flavored apricot sauce separately.

2587—VALENCIENNES TIMBALE OF PEARS
Timbale de Poires à la Valenciennes

Two-thirds fill a buttered *Charlotte-mould* with Savarin paste (2371). Let the paste rise by fermentation; bake it, and let it cool.

Remove the top which acts as a cover, and put it aside; then remove all of the soft crumb from the inside, leaving only the outside crust, and coat it with apricot syrup. Decoraté with alternate bands of sugar grains and chopped, very green pistachios.

Brush the cover with apricot syrup and decorate it in the same way. Quarter some "Duchesse," Beurré," "Doyenné," "Bartlett" or other creamy pears; peel them; cut them into somewhat thick slices, and cook them in butter after the manner of Pommes à Charlotte (2436). When the pears are well cooked, mix with them a quarter of their weight of apricot jam, and flavor with vanilla liqueur.

Serve the *timbale* with this preparation; put its cover on, and set it on a warm dish.

Serve a Kirsch-flavored apricot sauce (2410) separately.

APPLES (POMMES)

2588—APPLE FRITTERS   *Beignets de Pommes*

Take some russet apples, which are the best for the purpose, and make a hole through their centers with a corer. Peel them and cut them into round slices one-third of an inch thick, and steep them for twenty minutes in powdered sugar and brandy or rum.

A few minutes before serving, dry them slightly; dip the slices into thin batter, and plunge them into plenty of hot fat. Drain them, set them on a tray, sprinkle them with icing sugar, *glaze* them quickly, and serve them on a napkin.

2589—APPLES WITH BUTTER   *Pommes au Beurre*

Core some gray Calville baldwins, pippins or russet apples; peel them and parboil them for two minutes in boiling water, containing a little lemon juice. Then set them in a buttered saucepan; add a few tablespoons of vanilla-flavored syrup, and cook them covered in the oven. Serve them on little, round, brioche *croûtons, glazed* in the oven, and fill the hollow with butter kneaded with an equal weight of powdered sugar, and mixed with a little brandy.

Cover the apples with their own syrup, slightly thickened with apricot *purée*.

2590—BONNE-FEMME APPLES   *Pommes Bonne-Femme*

Core some russet apples and slightly cut them all round.

Place on a dish; fill the hollow of each with butter and powdered sugar mixed; pour a little water into the dish, and gently cook the apples in the oven.

Serve these apples as they stand.

2591—BOURDALOUE APPLES *Pommes Bourdaloue*

Quarter, peel and trim the apples, and cook them in vanilla-flavored syrup, keeping them somewhat firm. Proceed for the rest of the operation as directed under (2549).

2592—APPLE CHARLOTTE *Pommes en Charlotte*

See (2436).

2593—CHATELAINE APPLES *Pommes Châtelaine*

Take some medium-sized apples, and prepare them like those of (2590). Set them on a buttered dish; fill the hollow in each with a *salpicon* of half-sugared cherries, combined with apricot *purée;* cover with thin, *frangipan* cream; sprinkle with crushed sponge cake and macaroons and melted butter, and set the *gratin* to form in a hot oven.

2594—CHEVREUSE APPLES *Pommes Chevreuse*

On a dish, set a bed of a preparation for semolina croquettes (2453). All round arrange a close border of quartered apples cooked in vanilla-flavored syrup; fill the center with a *salpicon* of candied fruit and raisins, combined with an apricot *purée,* and cover with a thin coat of semolina.

Cover the whole with ordinary *meringue,* peaked; sprinkle some chopped pistachios upon the latter; dredge with icing sugar, and set to brown in a mild oven.

On taking the dish out of the oven decorate the top of the peak with a rosette of elongated angelica diamonds; place a small apple, cooked in pink syrup, in the middle of the rosette, and surround the base of the dessert with a circle of alternated white and pink, quartered apples.

2595—CONDE APPLES *Pommes Condé*

Poach some fine, peeled and trimmed apples in vanilla-flavored syrup. Serve them on a border of rice, decorated with cherries and angelica, as explained under (2551).

2596—GRATIN APPLES *Pommes Gratinées*

Set the quartered apples, *poached* in vanilla-flavored syrup, upon a base of minced apples prepared as for a *Charlotte* and kept somewhat stiff. Cover with fairly thin *pralin à Condé;* sprinkle with icing sugar, and place the dish in a mild oven, that the *pralin* may dry and color slightly.

2597—MERINGUED APPLES   *Pommes Meringuées*

Set the quartered apples, *poached* in vanilla-flavored syrup, upon a base of rice for croquettes, or of a mince as for a *Charlotte*. Cover with ordinary *meringue,* and smooth the latter, giving it the shape of a dome or a *Charlotte;* decorate with the same *meringue;* sprinkle with icing sugar, and bake and brown in a mild oven.

2598—MUSCOVITE APPLES   *Pommes Muscovite*

Take some well-shaped apples, uniform in size; trim to within two-thirds of their height, and take out the pulp from their insides in such a way as to make each resemble a kind of case.

Poach these cases in a thin syrup, keeping the pulp somewhat firm; drain them well, and set them on a dish.

Fill them, one-third full, with a *purée* made from the apple pulp, and fill them up with a Kümmel-flavored, apple-*soufflé* preparation (2405).

Cook in a mild oven for twenty minutes.

2599—PARISIENNE APPLES   *Pommes à la Parisienne*

Proceed exactly as for (2584).

2600—PORTUGUESE APPLES   *Pommes à la Portugaise*

Make cases of the apples as under (2598), and *poach* them in the same way, keeping them somewhat firm.

Fill them with stiff *frangipan* cream, combined with grated orange rind, crushed macaroons, and currants and sultana raisins (both washed and plumped in a Curaçao-flavored, lukewarm syrup).

Arrange these filled apples on a base of semolina-croquette (2453) preparation, and set them in the oven for ten minutes. On taking them out of the oven, coat their surface with melted red currant jelly, combined with a fine *julienne* of well-parboiled orange-*zest*.

2601—APPLE DUMPLING OR DOUILLON NORMAN
Rabotte de Pommes ou Douillon Norman

Prepare the apples like those "à la Bonne-femme" (2590), and enclose each in a layer of fine, short paste. Cover each dumpling with a scalloped round slice of the same paste; brush with egg; streak with a fork, and bake in a hot oven for fifteen minutes.

2602—APPLES IRENE   *Pommes Irène*

Select some nice apples; peel them, and cook them in syrup, keeping them somewhat firm. When they are cold, carefully remove their pulp, that they may form cases.

Rub the pulp through a sieve, sugar it with vanilla sugar (2438), and spread a layer of it on the bottom of each apple. Fill up the apple-cases with vanilla ice, combined with a *purée* of cooked plums; the proportions being one-third of the latter to one of the former.

Cover this ice with Kirsch-flavored Italian *meringue* (2383); set the latter to brown quickly, and serve instantly.

2603—NINON HOT APPLE PIE   *Flan de Pommes Chaud Ninon*

Prepare a baked pie crust without browning. Fill it with apples stewed as for a *Charlotte,* and shape these in the form of a dome. Upon these stewed apples set pink and white quartered apples, alternating the latter regularly; and, with a brush delicately coat these quarters of apple with some reduced white syrup.

2604—APPLE PIE A LA BATELIERE   *Flan de Pommes à la Batelière*

Line a spring form with some short paste, and fill it with apples, stewed as for a *Charlotte.*

Cover the apples with a dome of somewhat creamy rice for desserts, combined with the whites of four eggs beaten to a stiff froth per lb. of cooked rice.

Bake the deep pie in the usual way, and, on taking it out of the oven, sprinkle it copiously with icing sugar, and *glaze* with a red-hot iron.

VARIOUS HOT DESSERTS

2605—MINCE PIES   *Mince Pies*

Ingredients.—One lb. of chopped beef suet; one and one-third lbs. of cold, cooked fillet of beef, cut into very small dice; one lb. of seeded raisins; one lb. of currants and an equal quantity of sultana raisins; one lb. of candied peel; half lb. of peeled and chopped raw apples; the chopped *zest* and the juice of an orange; two-thirds oz. of allspice; one-sixth pint of brandy; and the same measure of Madeira and rum.

Thoroughly mix the whole; pour it into an earthenware jar; cover the latter, and let the preparation steep for a month.

Preparation.—Line some deep, buttered *tartlet moulds* with ordinary short paste; fill them with the above preparation; cover with a thin layer of puff-paste, having a hole in its centre; seal down this layer, brush with egg, and bake in a hot oven.

2606—CELESTINE OMELET   *Omelette Célestine*

Make an omelet from two eggs, and fill it either with cream, stewed fruit or jam. Make a somewhat larger omelet, and stuff it with a different filling from the one already used; enclose the first omelet in the second, and roll the latter up in the usual way. Sprinkle with icing sugar, and *glaze* in the oven or with a red-hot iron.

2607—EGGS A LA RELIGIEUSE   *Oeufs à la Religieuse*

Bake a somewhat deep pie-crust without browning, and have it of a size in proportion to the number of eggs it has to hold. Coat it inside with a layer of *pralin,* and dry the latter well in a mild oven.

Meanwhile *poach* the required number of fresh eggs in boiling milk, sugared to the extent of a quarter lb. per quart, and keep them somewhat soft. Drain them, and set them in the crust. Between each egg place a small slice of pineapple, cut to the shape of a cock's comb. Thicken the *poaching*-milk with five eggs and six egg-yolks per quart; pass it through a strainer: pour the preparation over the eggs, and put the deep pie in a mild oven, that the cream may be *poached* and slightly browned.

2608—GILDED CRUST (PAIN PERDU)   *Pain Perdu*

Cut some slices one-half inch thick from a brioche or a stale loaf of bread and dip them in cold sugared and vanilla-flavored milk. Drain the slices; dip them in some slightly-sugared beaten eggs, and place them in a frying-pan containing some very hot clarified butter (175). Brown them on both sides; drain them; sprinkle them with vanilla sugar, and serve them on a napkin.

2609—GABRIELLE FRUIT SUPREME   *Suprême de Fruits Gabrielle*

Prepare a border of apples, stewed as for a *Charlotte* thickened with eggs, and *poached* in a buttered and ornamented border mould.

Also a *macédoine* of fruit, the quantity of which should be in proportion to the capacity of the mould and consisting of quartered pears, cooked in syrup; pineapple, cut into large diamonds; half-sugared cherries; angelica, stamped into leaf-shapes by means of the fancy-cutter; and currants and sultana raisins, plumped in syrup. Set all these fruits in a saucepan.

To every pint of the pear-syrup add one lb. of sugar, and cook the mixture to the *small-ball* (236° F.) stage. This done, reduce it by

adding one-sixth pint of very thick almond milk (2506); pour this
over the fruit, and simmer very gently for ten minutes. Turn out
the border of apples, *poached* in a *bain-marie* (water-bath), upon a
dish, and surround it with a border of candied cherries. Complete
the *macédoine* away from the fire with a little very best butter;
pour it into the border, and sprinkle on it some peeled and finely-
slivered almonds.

2610—JEWISH SCHALETH   *Schâleth à la Juive*

Line a greased iron saucepan, or a large mould for "Pommes
Anna," with a thin layer of ordinary noodle paste (2291), and fill it
up with the following preparation:—For a utensil large enough to
hold one and a half quarts:—one and three quarter lbs. of thickly
stewed russet apples; one and a quarter lbs. in all of seeded Malaga
raisins, currants, and sultana raisins (plumped in tepid water) in
equal quantities; the finely grated *zests* of half an orange and a
half lemon; a bit of grated nutmeg; four oz. of powdered sugar; four
whole eggs and the yolks of six; and a quarter of a pint of Malaga
wine. Mix the whole well, in advance.

Cover with a layer of the noodle paste; seal the latter well down
round the edges; brush with egg, and make a slit in the top for the
escape of steam. Bake it in a moderate oven for fifty minutes, and
let it rest ten minutes before turning it out.

2611—ENGLISH FRUIT TARTS   *Tartes de Fruits à l'Anglaise*

These tarts are made in deep pie or pastry-dishes or forms. Whatever be the fruit used, clean it, peel it, or core it, according to its
nature. Some fruits are sliced while others are merely quartered or
left whole.

Set them in the dish, to within half inch of its brim; sprinkle them
with moist or powdered sugar, and (in the case of fruit with firm
pulps like apples) with a few tablespoons of water.

This addition of water is optional and, in any case, may be dispensed with for very juicy fruits. First cover the edges of the dish,
which should be moistened slightly, with a strip of short paste, an
inch wide. Then cover the dish with a layer of puff-paste, which
seal down well to the strip of paste, already in position and slightly
moistened for the purpose. With a brush moisten the layer of paste
constituting the cover of the tart; sprinkle it with sugar, and set
the tart to bake in a moderate oven.

All English tarts are made in this way, and all fruits may be used with them even when, as in the case of gooseberries, they are green.

Accompany these tarts by a sauceboat of fresh-cream or by a custard pudding (2406).

2612—SAUCES AND ACCOMPANIMENT OF COLD SWEETS
Sauces et Accompagnements d'Entremets Froids

Cold sweets allow of the following sauces:—

English Custard (2397), flavored according to taste.

Syrups of apricot, of mirabelle plums, of greengages, of red-currant, etc., the particular flavor of which should always be intensified by the addition of a liqueur in keeping with the fruit forming the base of the syrup. Kirsch and Maraschino are admirably suited to this purpose.

Purées of fresh fruit, such as strawberries, raspberries, red-currants, etc., combined with a little powdered sugar, and used plain or mixed with a little whipped cream.

Chantilly or Whipped Cream, flavored as taste may suggest.

Finally, certain desserts permit of the following sauce:—

2613—CHERRY SAUCE   *Sauce aux Cerises*

Gently melt one lb. of raspberry-flavored red-currant jelly. Pour it into a cold bowl, and add to it an equal quantity of freshly-prepared cherry juice, the juice of two blood-oranges, a little powdered ginger, and a few drops of carmine; the latter with the view of giving the preparation a sufficiently strong and distinctive color. Finally add a quarter of a lb. of half-sugared cherries, softened in a tepid, Kirsch-flavored syrup (2418).

BAVARIAN CREAMS

These are of two kinds:—

Bavarian with cream, and Bavarian with fruit.

2614—BAVARIAN CREAM   *Bavarois*

Preparation: Work one lb. of granulated sugar with fourteen egg-yolks in a saucepan, dilute with a pint and a half of boiled milk, in which a stick of vanilla has previously been steeped, and two-thirds of an oz. of gelatine dipped in cold water.

Put the preparation on a mild fire until it properly coats the withdrawn spoon, and do not let it boil. Pass it through the strainer into an enamelled bowl; let it cool, stirring it from time to time; and, when it begins to thicken, add one and a half pints of whipped cream, three oz. of powdered sugar, and two-thirds oz. of vanilla sugar (2349).

2615—BAVARIAN CREAM WITH FRUITS _Bavarois aux Fruits_

Ingredients.—One pint of fruit _purée_ diluted with one pint of syrup at 30° (saccharom.). Add the juice of three lemons, one oz. of dissolved gelatine, strained through linen, and one pint of whipped cream. The preparation for fruit Bavarians may be combined with fruit of the same nature as that used for the _purée;_ and this fruit may be added raw in the case of strawberries, raspberries, red-currants, etc., and _poached_ in the case of pulpy fruits, such as pears, peaches, apricots, etc.

2616—THE MOULDING AND DRESSING OF BAVARIAN CREAM
Moulage et Dressage de Bavarois

Bavarian creams are generally moulded in fancy moulds fitted with a central tube, slightly greased with sweet almond oil. When they are greased they are incrusted in cracked ice after the preparation has been covered with a round sheet of white paper.

When about to serve, the mould is quickly plunged into tepid water, wiped, and turned out upon a dish, which may or may not be covered with a folded napkin.

Instead of oiling the moulds they may be covered with a thin coat of sugar cooked to the _caramel_ (360° F.) stage, which besides making the Bavarian cream appetizing, also gives it an excellent taste. Another very advisable method is that of serving the Bavarian cream in a deep silver _timbale_ or dish, surrounded with ice. In this case, the dessert not having to be turned out, does not need to be so thick in consistency, and is therefore much more delicate.

When the Bavarian cream is served after this last method it is sometimes accompanied by stewed fruit or a _Macédoine_ of fresh fruit; though, in reality, these fruit accompaniments are better suited to cold puddings, which, in some points, are not unlike Bavarian creams.

Finally, when the Bavarian cream is moulded, it may be deco-rated, just before being served, with whipped cream piped on with a pastry-bag fitted with a fancy tube.

2617—CLERMONT BAVARIAN CREAM   *Bavarois Clermont*

Take some vanilla-flavored Bavarian cream preparation combined with three oz. of candied chestnut *purée* and three oz. of candied chestnuts, broken into small pieces, per pint of the preparation.

Having turned out the Bavarian cream, surround it with a crown of fine glacé chestnuts.

2618—DIPLOMAT BAVARIAN CREAM   *Bavarois Diplomate*

Coat a *timbale mould* with a layer of vanilla-flavored Bavarian cream preparation. Fill it with chocolate and strawberry Bavarian cream preparations, spread in alternate and regular layers.

2619—MY QUEEN BAVARIAN CREAM   *Bavarois My Queen*

Coat a Bavarian cream mould with a preparation of slightly-sugared fresh cream, combined with dissolved gelatine. Then fill up the mould with a Bavarian cream preparation, made from strawberry *purée* and combined with large strawberries, steeped in Kirsch. When the dessert is turned out surround it with a border of large strawberries, also steeped in sugar and Kirsch.

2620—BAVARIAN CREAM A LA RELIGIEUSE   *Bavarois à la Religieuse*

Coat a mould with some chocolate dissolved in a syrup containing a somewhat large proportion of gelatine. Fill the inside of the mould with a vanilla-flavored Bavarian cream preparation, made from plain instead of whipped cream.

2621—"RUBANNE" BAVARIAN CREAM   *Bavarois Rubanné*

This kind of Bavarian cream is made from differently-colored and differently-flavored preparations, spread in alternate layers in the mould.

It is therefore governed by no hard and fast rules, and every kind of Bavarian cream preparation may be used.

2622—VARIOUS BAVARIAN CREAMS   *Bavarois Divers*

Almond, anisette, filbert, coffee, chocolate, Kirsch, fresh walnut, orange, and violet Bavarian creams, etc., may be prepared after (2614); the flavor alone undergoing any change.

2623—VARIOUS FRUIT BAVARIAN CREAMS
Bavarois aux Fruits Divers

After the general recipe, Bavarian cream may be prepared from pineapple, apricots, strawberries, raspberries, melon, etc.

2624—BLANC-MANGE
Blanc-Manger

Blanc-mange is scarcely ever served nowadays, and this is a pity; seeing that, when it is well prepared, it is one of the best desserts that can be set before a diner. Blanc-mange, as it is prepared in England, is quite different from that generally served; but it is nevertheless an excellent and very wholesome dessert, and that is why I have given its recipe below.

As a matter of fact, in order to justify its name, blanc-mange ought always to be beautifully white; but, for a long time since, the compound word has lost its original meaning. The adjective and noun composing it have fused one with the other to form a single general title, which may now be applied with equal propriety to both colored and white preparations; and the verbal error is so old, dating as it does from pre-Carême times, that it would be futile to try and correct it.

2625—FRENCH BLANC-MANGE
Blanc-Manger à la Française

Preparation.—Skin one lb. of sweet almonds and four or five bitter almonds, and soak them well in fresh water that they may be quite white.

Pound them as finely as possible; adding to them a spoonful at a time, one pint of water. Strain the whole through a strong towel, twisting the latter tightly; melt one lb. of sugar in the almond milk (about one and half pints); add a scant oz. of gelatine dissolved in tepid syrup; strain the whole through muslin, and flavor according to taste.

Moulding:—Mould the blanc-mange in oiled moulds with center-tubes (funnels) as for Bavarian creams. Incrust them in ice that their contents may set, and proceed for the turning-out as already directed.

N.B.—For the preparation of almond milk, modern Cookery has substituted for the procedure given above, which is antiquated, another which consists in pounding the almonds with only a few tablespoons of water and some very thin cream.

2626—BLANC-MANGE WITH FRUIT AND LIQUEURS
Blancs-Mangers aux Fruits et aux Liqueurs

All fruits, reduced to *purées,* may serve in the preparation of blanc-manges, and the apportioning of the ingredients should be as follows. The *purée* of the selected fruit and the preparation given above (including the same amount of gelatine) should be mixed in equal quantities.

These blanc-manges take the name of the fruit with which they are prepared: strawberries, raspberries, apricots, peaches, etc. They may also be prepared with liqueurs, which should be in the proportion of one liqueur glass to one quart of the preparation. The best liqueurs for the purpose are Kirsch, Maraschino and Rum.

Blanc-manges are also made from chocolate and coffee, although the flavor of the latter does not blend so well with that of almonds as do the other products.

2627—BLANC-MANGES "RUBANNES" *Blanc-Mangers Rubannés*

Prepare these as directed under (2621), spreading the differently flavored and colored blanc-mange preparations in alternate even and regular layers.

N.B.—Blanc-mange preparations may also be served in silver *timbales,* in good china or glass dishes, or in deep pie dishes. By this means, to the great improvement of the preparation, the gelatine may be reduced to a minimum quantity, just enough to ensure the setting of the blanc-mange and no more. And the thing is quite possible inasmuch as there is no question of turning out the dessert.

In his book "The Parisian Cook," Carême recommends the addition to the Blanc-mange of a quarter of its volume of very fresh, good cream; and the advice, coming as it does from such an authoritative source, is worth following.

2628—ENGLISH BLANC-MANGE *Blanc-Manger à l'Anglaise*

Boil one quart of milk, containing four oz. of sugar, and pour it over a quarter of a lb. of corn meal diluted with half a pint of cold milk; stirring briskly the while.

Smooth the preparation with the whisk, and cook it over an open fire for a few minutes, without ceasing to stir.

On taking it off the fire, flavor it according to taste; and pour it, very hot, into moulds previously moistened with syrup, that the mouldings may turn out glossy and smooth.

Let the contents of the moulds set; turn them out, and serve them very cold either plain or with an accompaniment of stewed fruit.

CHARLOTTES

2629—HARLEQUIN CHARLOTTE *Charlotte à l'Arléquine*

Line the bottom of a *Charlotte mould* with a round piece of paper, and fill the sides with upright pieces of *Génoise, glazed* white, pink and pale-green; alternating the colors and pressing them snugly one against the other. Meanwhile, take some strawberry, chocolate, pistachio and apricot Bavarian cream preparations, and let them set in flat spring forms, lying on pieces of oiled paper.

Cut the Bavarian cream preparations into large dice, and mix them with an ordinary, and somewhat liquid, Bavarian cream preparation. Pour the whole into the mould, and leave to cool. When about to serve, turn out the *Charlotte;* remove the piece of paper and replace it by a thin *Génoise* top, *glazed* with "fondant" (2346) and decorated with candied fruit.

2630—CARMEN CHARLOTTE *Charlotte Carmen*

Line the *Charlotte* with thin wafers, and fill it with the following preparation:—eight oz. of stewed tomatoes; four oz. of stewed red-sweet peppers, a pinch of powdered ginger, three oz. of candied ginger cut into dice, the juice of three lemons, half a pint of hot syrup at 32° (saccharom.), and about three ounces of dissolved gelatine.

Mix up the whole, and, when the preparation begins to thicken, add to it one and three-quarter pints of whipped cream.

2631—CHANTILLY (WHIPPED CREAM) CHARLOTTE *Charlotte Chantilly*

Prepare the *Charlotte* with *gaufrettes* (thin wafers), stuck directly upon a round base of dry paste, either with apricot jam cooked to the *small-thread* stage (215° F.) or with sugar cooked to the *small-crack* stage (285° F.). As a help, a *Charlotte mould* may be used for this operation; it may be laid on the dry-paste base and removed when the *gaufrettes* are all stuck.

Garnish with whipped, sugared and vanilla-flavored cream built up in pyramid-form, and decorate its surface, by means of a spoon, with the same cream, slightly tinted with pink.

2632—BUCKET AND BASKET WITH WHIPPED CREAM *Baquet et Panier Chantilly*

A "bucket" is made with sponge lady's finger, well trimmed and stuck upon a base of dry paste with sugar cooked to the *large-crack* stage (315° F.).

In the middle, and on either side of the bucket, set a "lady finger," somewhat higher than the rest, with a hole in its top end, cut by means of a small round cutter; and surround the bucket with small bands of chocolate-flavored almond paste, in imitation of iron hoops.

The "basket" is made in the same way, but with sponge "lady fingers" all of the same size, and without the imitation iron-hoops. On the base and by means of sugar cooked to the *large-crack* stage (315° F.), fix a handle of pulled sugar, decorated with sugar flowers.

The "bucket" and the "basket" are filled with the same cream as the Chantilly Charlotte, and are finished in the same way, with a decoration of pink-tinted cream.

2633—MONTREUIL CHARLOTTE   *Charlotte Montreuil*

Line the bottom and sides of the mould with sponge lady fingers. Fill with a Bavarian cream preparation consisting of one pint of peach *purée* per quart of English custard (2624), and the usual quantity of whipped cream.

Add some very ripe, sliced and sugared peaches, on putting the preparation into the mould.

2634—OPERA CHARLOTTE   *Charlotte Opéra*

Line a mould with Perfetto or Nabisco sugar wafers and garnish it with a vanilla-flavored Bavarian cream preparation, combined with one-quarter of its bulk of a smooth *purée* of glacé chestnuts, and a *salpicon* of candied fruit, steeped in Maraschino.

2635—PLOMBIERE CHARLOTTE   *Charlotte Plombière*

Line the Charlotte with sponge lady fingers or with *gaufrettes*. When about to serve, garnish it with a Plombière ice (2795) and turn it out upon a napkin.

2636—RENAISSANCE CHARLOTTE   *Charlotte Renaissance*

Line the bottom of the mould with a round piece of white paper, and the sides with rectangles of *Génoise, glazed* white and pink. Set the *glazed* sides of the rectangles against the mould.

Fill the mould, thus lined, with a vanilla-flavored Bavarian cream preparation, combined with raw peeled and sliced apricots and peaches, pineapple cut into dice, and wild strawberries, all these fruits having been previously steeped in Kirsch. Let the preparation set in a cool place or on ice.

When the *Charlotte* is turned out, remove the round piece of paper, and in its place lay a slice of pineapple, cut from the thickest part of the fruit and decorated with candied fruit.

2637—CHARLOTTE RUSSE
Charlotte Russe

Make a rosette on the bottom of the mould with some heart-shaped sponge lady fingers, and line the sides with the same, trimmed, set upright and close together.

This *Charlotte* may be filled with a vanilla-, *pralin-*, coffee-, orange- or chocolate-flavored Bavarian cream preparation; or a Bavarian cream preparation made from a *purée* of such fruits as apricots, pineapple, bananas, peaches, strawberries, etc.

The flavor or product which determines the character of the *Charlotte* should always be referred to on the menu, thus: *Charlotte Russe à l'Orange* or *Charlotte Russe aux Fraises,* etc.

2638—CREAMS
Crèmes

Cold creams, served as desserts, belong to two very distinct classes: *Cooked Creams,* which are, in short, but a variety of custard.

The Creams derived from natural, fresh cream, whipped and sugared, the general type of which is Chantilly cream (2402).

Cooked Creams are prepared either in special little pots, in small silver or porcelain bowls, or in moulds. Those prepared in moulds are turned out when they are quite cold, and are called *"Crèmes renversées"* to distinguish them from the first two kinds which are always served in the utensil in which they have cooked.

For all that, the term *"Crème renversée"* has grown somewhat obsolete, and the modern expression for this kind of custard is *"Crème moulée."*

Crème au Caramel represents a perfect type of this class.

The custards served in their cooking-receptacles are more delicate than the others, because their preparation does not demand such a large quantity of eggs; but they are only served in the home. For a stylish luncheon or dinner, moulded custards (Fr. crèmes moulées) are best.

2639—MOULDED VANILLA CREAM
Crème Moulée à la Vanille

Boil one quart of milk containing one-half lb. of sugar; add a stick of vanilla, and let the latter steep for twenty minutes. Pour this milk, little by little, over three eggs and eight yolks, previously beaten in a bowl, and whisk briskly. Pass the whole through a fine sieve; let it rest for a moment or two; then completely remove all the froth on its surface, and pour the preparation into buttered custard cups or into little covered pots specially made for this purpose. Set to *poach* in a *bain-marie* (water-bath), in a moderate oven, keeping lids on the utensils.

Not for one moment must the water in the *bain-marie* boil while
the *poaching* is in progress; for the air contained by the preparation
would then become over-heated, and the result would be an innumerable amount of small holes throughout the depth of the
custard, which would greatly mar its appearance.

As a matter of fact, the custard should *poach,* that is to say, coagu-
late, as the result of the surrounding water being kept at a constant
temperature of 185° F. As soon as it is *poached,* let the custard cool.

When it is *poached* in the utensils in which it is served, one egg
and eight yolks per quart of milk will be found sufficient. The utensils should be carefully wiped and placed on a napkin.

If the custard is to be turned out, carefully overturn the custard
cup upon a dish, and pull it off a few minutes later. Moulded and
potted custards permit of all the flavorings proper to desserts;
but those which suit them best are vanilla, almond milk, almond
and filbert *pralin,* coffee, chocolate, etc. Unless used in the form
of very concentrated *essences,* fruit flavors are less suited to them.

2640—MOULDED CARAMEL CREAM   *Crème Moulée au Caramel*

Coat the bottom and sides of a mould with sugar cooked to the
golden-caramel stage (360° F.), and fill it up with a vanilla-flavored,
moulded-custard preparation. *Poach* and turn it out as directed.

2641—VIENNA MOULDED CREAM   *Crème Moulée à la Viennoise*

This is a custard with caramel, but instead of coating the mould
with the latter, it is dissolved in the hot milk. The custard should
be treated exactly like the vanilla-flavored kind.

2642—FLORENTINE MOULDED CREAM   *Crème Moulée à la Florentine*

Make a preparation of *pralin*-flavored custard with caramel and
poach it.

When it is quite cold, turn it out on a dish; decorate it with
Kirsch-flavored whipped cream, and sprinkle its surface with
chopped pistachios.

2643—OPERA MOULDED CREAM   *Crème Moulée Opéra*

Poach, in an ornamented *border-mould,* a preparation of *pralin*-
flavored custard. When it is turned out, garnish its midst with a
dome of whipped cream, perfumed with *pralined* violets. Upon
the border set a crown of fine strawberries, steeped in a Kirsch-
flavored syrup, and cover with a veil of sugar cooked to the
large-crack stage (315° F.).

Cold Creams with a Whipped-Cream Base

2644—CHANTILLY CREAM   *Crème Chantilly*

Take some fresh and somewhat thick cream, and whisk it until it is sufficiently stiff to span the wires of the whisk. Add to it eight oz. of powdered sugar per quart of cream, and flavor with vanilla or fruit *essence.*

Whatever be the purpose of this cream, it should, if possible, be prepared only at the last moment.

2645—CHANTILLY WHIPPED CREAM WITH FRUIT

Crème Chantilly aux Fruits

The ingredients for this preparation are a *purée* of the selected fruit and whipped cream, in the proportion of one-third of the former to two-thirds of the latter.

The quantities of sugar and kind of flavor vary according to the nature of the fruit.

It is served either as a dessert garnish, or alone in a bowl, with a decoration of the same cream, piped with a pastry-bag fitted with a small even or grooved tube. Send some sponge lady fingers separately.

2646—CAPRICE CREAM   *Crème Caprice*

Take some whipped cream, and add to it one-quarter of its bulk of roughly broken-up *meringues.* Put the preparation in an iced *Madeleine-mould,* lined with white paper; seal up thoroughly; tie tightly, and keep the utensil in ice for two hours.

Turn out when about to serve; remove the paper; and decorate, with a pastry-bag fitted with a fancy tube, with whipped cream, tinted pink with strawberry and raspberry juice.

2647—BRISE DU PRINTEMPS (SPRINGTIME BREEZES)

Brise du Printemps

Take some violet-flavored, slightly-iced whipped cream, and set in small dessert-dishes, by means of a spoon.

2648—NUEES ROSES (SHOWER OF ROSES)   *Roses Nuées*

Take some whipped cream, scented with vanilla-flavored strawberry *purée,* and serve it in small dessert-dishes, by means of a spoon.

2649—FLAMRI *Flamri*

Boil one pint of white wine and as much water, and sprinkle in it eight oz. of small semolina. Cook gently for twenty-five minutes. Then add to the preparation two-thirds lb. of powdered sugar, a pinch of table-salt, two eggs, and the whites of six, beaten to a stiff froth.

Pour it into moulds with buttered sides; set these to *poach* in the *bain-marie* (water-bath), and leave them to cool. Turn out, and coat with a *purée* of raw fruit, such as strawberries, red-currants, cherries, etc., reasonably sugared.

2650—JELLIES *Gelées*

From the standpoint of their preparation, jellies are of two kinds: wine or liqueur-flavored jellies; or fruit jellies. But their base is the same in all cases, gelatine dissolved in a certain quantity of water.

The gelatine should be extracted from calf's foot, by boiling the latter; but, although this is the best that can be obtained, the means of obtaining it are the most complicated. The gelatine bought ready-made may also be used in the quantities given below.

2651—CALF'S-FOOT JELLY *Gelée de Pieds de Veau*

Take some fine soaked and *blanched* calves' feet, and set them to cook in one and three-quarters pints of water apiece. Skim as thoroughly as possible; cover, and then cook very gently for seven hours. This done, strain the cooking-liquor and clear it of all grease; test its strength, after having cooled a little of it on ice; correct it if too thick with sufficient filtered water, and once more test it by means of ice.

Per quart of calf's-foot jelly, add eight oz. of sugar, a bit of cinnamon, half the rind of an orange and lemon, and all their juice.

For the clarification, proceed as directed hereafter.

2652—JELLY WITH GELATINE BASE *Gelée à Base de Gélatine*

Dissolve one oz. of granulated gelatine in a quart of water. Add one-half lb. of sugar, one-sixth oz. of coriander, and the *zest* and juice of half a lemon and of a whole orange; boil, and then let the preparation stand for ten minutes away from the fire.

Whisk one and a half egg-whites in a very clean saucepan, together with a port wine-glass of white wine, and pour the cleared syrup, little by little, over the egg-whites, whisking briskly the while. Set the saucepan on the fire, and continue whisking until the boil is reached; then move the utensil to a corner of the stove, and keep the jelly only just simmering for one-quarter of an hour.

At the end of that time the clarification is completed; strain the jelly through a bag, placed over a very clean bowl, and, if the jelly is cloudy after the first time of straining, strain it again and again until it becomes quite clear. Let it almost cool before adding any flavor.

The Flavoring.—Whether the jelly be prepared from calves' feet or from gelatine, the above preparation is nothing more than a combined syrup, to which the addition of some flavor lends the character of a jelly. The complementary ingredients for jellies are liqueurs, good wines, and the juice of fruit; and the quantity of water prescribed should be so reduced as to allow for the ultimate addition of the liquid flavoring.

Thus, every jelly of which the flavor is a liqueur ought to be prepared with only nine-tenths of a quart of water; and the remaining one-tenth of the measure is subsequently added in the form of Kirsch, Maraschino, Rum, or Anisette, etc.

A jelly flavored with a good wine, such as Champagne, Madeira, Sherry, Marsala, etc., should contain only seven-tenths of a quart of water and three-tenths of a quart of the selected wine.

In the case of *fruit jellies,* the procedure differs in accordance with the kind of fruit used.

For *red-fruit jellies,* prepared from strawberries, raspberries, red-currants, cherries, and canberries, these fruits, which should be very ripe, are rubbed through a sieve, and combined with one-tenth to three-tenths of a quart of water per lb., according to whether the fruit be more or less juicy.

This done, filter the resulting juice, and add it to the jelly in the proportion of one part of the former to two parts of the latter. The jelly should therefore be twice as strong as for the previous preparation, in order that it may remain sufficiently consistent in spite of the added juice.

When the fruit is too juicy, rub it through a sieve; let the juice ferment for a few hours, and only filter the clear juice which results from the fermentation.

Juicy-fruit jellies, prepared from grapes, oranges, lemons, and tangerines, are made in the same way. The filtering of these fruit juices is easily done, and, except for the grapes, they need not be set to ferment.

When these fruits are not quite ripe, their juices may be added

to the jelly even before the clarification—a procedure which helps
to modify their acidity. The apportionment of the fruit juices to
the jelly is practically the same as that of the red-fruit juices.

Stone-fruit, such as apricots, peaches, nectarines, plums, etc., are
often used as jelly garnishes, but seldom serve as the flavoring base
of a jelly. Whenever they are treated in this way, they are first
plunged in boiling water, that they may be peeled; they are then
poached and left to cool in the syrup which goes towards preparing
the jelly.

This jelly, after it has been clarified and three-parts cooled, should
have a little Kirsch or Maraschino added to it, that its fruit flavor
may be intensified.

2653—THE GARNISH AND ACCOMPANIMENTS OF JELLY
Garnitures et Accompagnement des Gelées

As a rule, jellies are served plain. Sometimes, however, they are
garnished with variously-shaped, stewed fruits, symmetrically distributed in the jelly, with their colors nicely contrasted.

A jelly prepared in this way is called a "Suédoise of fruit."

2654—"RUBANE" JELLY   *Gelées Rubanées*

These are differently-flavored and differently-colored jellies
moulded in alternate layers, even and equally thick.

They are generally served without garnish.

2655—JELLY A LA RUSSE   *Les Gelées à la Russe*

These are ordinary jellies which are whisked over ice until they
begin to set. They are then speedily moulded. By skilfully mixing
two or three of these jellies, of different shades and flavors, at
the moment of moulding, very effective "Marbled Jellies" are
obtained.

2656—JELLY A LA MUSCOVITE   *Les Gelées à la Muscovite*

These are ordinary jellies, poured into tightly-closing moulds,
the sealing of which is ensured by a thread of butter, laid round
the edges of the lids. The moulds are then surrounded with cracked
ice, mixed with five lb. of freezing salt and eight oz. of saltpetre
per twenty-five lb. of ice.

The cold produced by the salted ice causes a frosted coat to form
round the jelly, the effect of which is exceedingly pretty. But the
moulds should be removed from the ice as soon as the frosted coat

is formed and the jelly is set; for a longer time in the cold would transform the jelly into an uneatable block of ice.

N.B.—Modern methods have greatly simplified the dishing and serving of jellies. They are now served in special silver bowls or deep dishes, and they are not, as a rule, moulded. The bottom of these utensils is sometimes decorated with stewed fruit or *macédoines* of fruit which are covered with the jelly; and, as the latter is served in the utensil itself, the quantity of gelatine may be reduced, and greater delicacy is the result.

2657—FRUIT LOAVES *Pains de Fruits*

These "pains" (loaves) are made in ordinary *Charlotte*-moulds.

Coat the mould with a fairly thick layer of jelly, in keeping with the flavor of the fruit used, which may be apricots, strawberries, red-currants, cherries, peaches, etc. Fill up the mould with a preparation, made as for a fruit Bavarian, but without cream.

The amount of gelatine used should therefore be reduced.

2658—COLD PUDDINGS *Puddings Froids*

Cold puddings have a great deal in common with Bavarians and, more often than not, these two kinds of desserts have the same base. Their distinguishing difference lies in the fact that Bavarians are generally served without a garnish or sauce, whereas puddings always have either one or the other, and sometimes both.

The sauces for puddings are those given at the beginning of this chapter.

Their garnishes always consist of fruit, and the latter is either stewed and served separately, or it is candied and combined with the pudding paste.

2659—BOHEMIENNE PUDDING *Pudding Bohémienne*

Make some very small pancakes, and garnish them with a *salpicon* of candied fruits and currants plumped in tepid water, mixed with some fairly stiff, apple *purée*. Fold up the pancakes to the shape of balls or rectangles, and set them in a buttered border-mould. Fill up the mould with a moulded-custard preparation (2639), containing a good proportion of whole eggs, and *poach* in a *bain-marie* (water-bath).

Leave the whole to cool in the mould; turn out at the last moment, and coat the pudding with a *sabayon*, flavored according to taste.

2660—DIPLOMAT PUDDING *Pudding Diplomate*

Decorate the bottom of an oiled deep Bavarian cream mould with pieces of candied fruit. Fill up the mould with alternate layers of vanilla-flavored Bavarian cream preparation and sponge lady fingers, saturated with Kirsch. On each layer of "lady-fingers" sprinkle some currants and raisins plumped in tepid water, and here and there place a tablespoon of apricot jam.

Let the contents of the mould set in a cool place or on ice, and turn out just before serving.

2661—DIPLOMAT FRUIT PUDDING *Pudding Diplomate aux Fruits*

Prepare the pudding as above, but spread a few extra layers of fresh fruit in the mould, such as very ripe pears, peaches, apricots, etc., all peeled, cut into thin slices, and previously steeped with powdered sugar and half a port wine-glass of either Kirsch, Maraschino, or Anisette, etc.

When the pudding is turned out, surround its base with some very cold stewed fruit the same as one of the kinds used inside the pudding, or some stewed, mixed fruit.

2662—MALAKOFF PUDDING *Pudding Malakoff*

Prepare a gelatinous English custard (2397), combined with one pint of very fresh cream per quart; a stew of apples and pears, prepared as for an apple *Charlotte;* currants and sultana raisins, plumped in tepid syrup; fresh slivered almonds; candied orange peel, cut into dice; slices of stale sponge cake, or sponge lady fingers, saturated with liqueur. Oil a *Charlotte* mould, and pour into it a layer of cream half an inch thick. Upon this cream lay a thickness of sponge cake or lady fingers, copiously coated with marmalade, and sprinkle with raisins, almonds and orange peel dice.

Cover with a layer of cream; lay a second thickness of sponge cake and proceed thus in the same order with a Kirsch-flavored cold *sabayon.*

2663—NESSELRODE PUDDING *Pudding Nesselrode*

To an English custard, prepared after (2397), add eight oz. of a smooth, chestnut *purée,* and four oz. of currants and sultana raisins plumped in tepid water, and candied orange peel and cherries, cut into dice; these four products should be in almost equal quantities, and should have been previously steeped in sweetened Madeira.

Add some Maraschino-flavored, whipped cream to the prepara-tion; apportioning it as for a Bavarian cream.

Line the bottom and sides of a *Charlotte* mould with white paper; pour the preparation into the mould; completely close the latter, sealing the lid down with a thread of butter, and surround the utensil with plenty of salted ice. When about to serve, turn out on a napkin; remove the paper, and surround the base of the pudding with a crown of fine, glacé chestnuts, or balls of chocolate-iced, glacé chestnut *purée*.

N.B.—The English custard may be packed in the freezer, mixed with whipped cream when it is almost congealed, and then placed in a mould.

2664—RICHELIEU PUDDING *Pudding Richelieu*

Rub some stewed prunes through a fine sieve, and add to the *purée* equal quantities of very stiff, Kirsch-flavored jelly and the reduced juice of the prunes. Let a layer three-quarters of an inch thick, of the preparation set on the bottom of a *Charlotte* mould. In the latter set a small mould, filled with broken ice, and either fitted with handles that can rest on the brim of the first mould, or else sufficiently deep to be easily grasped and removed when neces-sary. The space between the sides of the two moulds should measure about three-quarters of an inch.

Fill up this space with what remains of the prune *purée*, thick-ened with jelly; leave the preparation to set; remove the ice from the little mould; pour some tepid water into the latter, that it may be immediately detached from the surrounding, iced preparation.

Fill the space left by the withdrawn mould with some vanilla-flavored Bavarian cream preparation; leave to set, and turn out at the last moment on a napkin.

2665—FAIRY QUEEN PUDDING OR CREAM

Pudding ou Crème Reine des Fées

Prepare the whites of four eggs as for Italian *meringue* (2383), and add to the sugar, while cooking, its bulk of quince jelly, and, at the last moment, one and a half ounces of candied fruit, cut into dice, steeped in Kirsch and carefully drained. Set the *meringue*, in shapes resembling large buttons, on a sheet of paper.

Boil in a utensil large enough to take the sheet of paper, four quarts of water, containing two and a half lb. of sugar and one-quarter pint of Kirsch. Slip the sheet of paper into this boiling syrup; withdraw it as soon as it easily separates from the pieces of *meringue; poach* them; drain them on a piece of linen and let them cool.

Meanwhile, make two Bavarian cream preparations; one white and vanilla-flavored, and the other pink and flavored with Curaçao. In these preparations the quantity of whipped cream should be twice as much as for ordinary Bavarian cream, whereas the quantity of gelatine should be reduced by half.

Set these preparations in even, alternate layers, in a slightly-oiled iced-*Madeleine mould,* distributing the *meringues* between each layer.

Cover the mould with a piece of paper and a lid, and keep it surrounded by ice for two hours. When about to serve, turn it out on a napkin.

COLD FRUIT ENTREMETS

Apricots (Abricots)

2666—PARISIENNE APRICOTS   *Abricots à la Parisienne*
Poach the halved apricots in vanilla-flavored syrup. Cool them and drain them; and reconstruct the apricots by joining the halves together with a piece of vanilla ice-cream, the size of a walnut, in the center.

Set these apricots upon some large overturned macaroons; cover with vanilla-flavored whipped cream, shaped like a cone and sprinkle with fine filbert *pralin.*

2667—ROYALE APRICOTS   *Abricots à la Royale*
Take some fairly deep *tartlet moulds,* and set in them some fine, cold, half-apricots, *poached* in vanilla-flavored syrup. Fill up the *tartlet* moulds with very transparent, Kirsch-flavored jelly.

Prepare a shallow, *Génoise* border, *glazed* with red-currant jelly, cooked to the *small-thread* stage (215° F.), and sprinkle with chopped pistachios.

Turn out the *tartlets* of apricot jelly and place them in a crown over the border. Fill the center of the latter with chopped anisette-flavored pink jelly.

PINEAPPLE (ANANAS)

2668—GEORGETTE PINEAPPLE *Ananas Georgette*

Take a fine pineapple, and hollow it out to within half an inch of its outside all round and at the bottom. Put aside the slice cut from the top, on which is the bunch of leaves.

Fill the inside with a Bavarian cream preparation made from pineapple *purée,* combined with the removed pineapple, cut into thin slices, and leave to set. Place on a napkin, and return the top slice to the pineapple, that it may seem untouched.

2669—VIRGINIA PINEAPPLE *Ananas Virginie*

Proceed exactly as above, but replace the pineapple Bavarian cream preparation by a strawberry kind, combined, as before, with the flesh removed from the inside of the pineapple, cut in dice.

2670—NINON PINEAPPLE *Ananas Ninon*

Line the sides of a *soufflé timbale* with vanilla ice-cream, laying it in an oblique strip from the edge of the utensil to the center of the bottom of the *timbale.* Upon this layer of ice-cream set two or three rows of thin pineapple slices, in such a way as to make the slices of the last row project beyond the edge of the *timbale.*

In the center of the mould build a pyramid of wild strawberries; cover this with a raspberry *purée,* and sprinkle with chopped pistachios.

2670a—ROYALE PINEAPPLE *Ananas à la Royale*

Take a fresh pineapple and cut a slice from its top, containing the bunch of leaves. Scoop the pulp from the inside, and leave a thickness of about half an inch all round and on the bottom.

Fill it with a *macédoine* of fresh fruit steeped in Kirsch; set it in the middle of a crystal bowl; and surround the base with a crown of fine peaches, *poached* in a vanilla-flavored syrup, alternated by large strawberries, steeped in Kirsch.

Return the bunch of leaves to its place upon the pineapple.

CHERRIES (CERISES)

2671—DU BARRY CHERRIES *Cerises DuBarry*

Line a small round spring form with good, short paste; set it on baking-sheet; prick the paste on the bottom to prevent its blistering while baking, sprinkle with powdered sugar, and fill with fine, pitted cherries, pressed snugly one against the other.

Bake the crust with cherries in the usual way and let it cool.

When it is quite cold cover the cherries with whipped cream, combined either with ordinary *pralin* or with crushed macaroons.

Smooth the surface of the cream, as also the sides of the crust; cover it with crushed powdered macaroon, and then decorate by means of the pastry-bag with white and pink whipped cream.

2672—CHERRIES IN CLARET   *Cerises au Vin Rouge*

Select some fine cherries; cut off the ends of their stems, and set them in a silver *timbale*. Pour sufficient sweetened Bordeaux wine (flavored with a bit of cinnamon) over them, to just cover them. Close the *timbale,* and keep it on the side of the fire for ten minutes, that the cherries may *poach.*

Let them cool in the syrup; drain the latter away; reduce it by a third, and add, in order to thicken it slightly, one tablespoon of red-currant jelly per six tablespoons of reduced syrup.

Serve the cherries quite cold, and some sponge lady fingers separately.

STRAWBERRIES (FRAISES)

2673—CREOLE STRAWBERRIES   *Fraises à la Créole*

Set some fine strawberries and an equal amount of pineapple, cut into dice, to steep in powdered sugar and Kirsch.

Arrange a close crown of pineapple slices, also steeped in Kirsch, upon a large shallow compote dish. In the middle of the crown build a pyramid of the strawberries and pineapple, and sprinkle with a Kirsch-flavored syrup.

2674—FEMINA STRAWBERRIES   *Fraises Fémina*

Select some fine strawberries; sprinkle them with sugar and Grand-Marnier Curaçao, and leave them to steep on ice for an hour.

When about to serve, spread on the bottom of a bowl or *timbale* a layer of orange-ice (which should be combined with the steeping liqueur) and set the strawberries on the ices.

2675—MARGUERITE STRAWBERRIES   *Fraises Marguerite*

Set some wild strawberries to steep in sugar and Kirsch. Drain them; combine them with an equal quantity of pomegranate sherbet; set them in a silver *timbale,* already surrounded with ice, cover the strawberries with Maraschino-flavored whipped cream, and decorate with the latter.

2676—MARQUISE STRAWBERRIES   *Fraises Marquise*
Set in a *timbale* surrounded with ice some whipped cream, combined with half its bulk of a *purée* of wild strawberries. Completely cover this cream with fine, fair-sized selected strawberries steeped with Kirsch, rolled at the last minute in granulated sugar.

2677—MELBA STRAWBERRIES   *Fraises Melba*
Fill the bottom of a *timbale* with vanilla ice-cream. Upon this arrange a layer of choice strawberries, and cover the latter with a thick, slightly-sugared, fresh raspberry *purée.*

2678—NINA STRAWBERRIES   *Fraises Nina*
Prepare the strawberries as directed under (2675), and mix them with pineapple sherbet. Serve them as before in a *timbale,* and cover them with some whipped cream, tinted pink with a red-pimento *purée* flavored with ginger.

2679—ROMANOFF STRAWBERRIES   *Fraises Romanoff*
Steep some fine strawberries with orange juice and Curaçao. Set them in a *timbale* surrounded with ice, and cover them with whipped cream, piped on with a pastry-bag, fitted with a large, grooved pipe.

2680—WILHELMINA STRAWBERRIES   *Fraises Wilhelmine*
Steep some fine, large strawberries with Kirsch, powdered sugar, and orange juice. Put them in a *timbale* and serve a vanilla-flavored whipped cream separately.

2681—LERINA STRAWBERRIES   *Fraises Lérina*
Take a small black melon of Carmes or a fine cantaloup; open it by cutting out a bung-shaped piece containing the stalk, and remove all its seeds. Then scoop out all the pulp, with a dessert-spoon, and sprinkle it with powdered sugar.

Steep the required number of strawberries in Lérina (Chartreuse) liqueur.

Fill the inside of the melon with these strawberries and the scooped out flesh; close the melon by replacing the bung cut out at the start, and keep in a refrigerator for two hours, surrounded by ice.

Serve on a napkin at the last moment.

2682—BABY'S DREAM STRAWBERRIES   *Fraises Rêve de Bébé*

Select a fair-sized, very ripe pineapple, cut off a slice of it at the top and scoop out all its flesh without breaking the rind.

Prepare a square bed of *Génoise,* about two inches thick; slightly hollow it out towards its center, that the emptied pineapple may be set upright upon it; and stick the cushion upon a dry-paste base, of the same size and shape as the former. *Glaze* the *Génoise* bed with pink *fondant,* decorate with "royale" *glaze,* and set a large strawberry at each corner.

Slice half of the scooped out pineapple flesh, and steep it with Kirsch, Maraschino and sugar. Pound the remaining pulp and press it in order to extract its juice.

Set to steep with this pineapple juice a sufficient quantity of strawberries to three-parts fill the pineapple.

When about to serve, fill the emptied pineapple with successive and alternate layers of pineapple with Kirsch and strawberries; and, between each layer, spread a coat of vanilla-flavored, whipped cream.

Close the pineapple with the slice cut off at the start, and set it upright in the hollow of the cake. Serve the preparation very cold.

2683—STRAWBERRIES A LA RITZ   *Fraises à la Ritz*

Put some well-sugared and cooled strawberries in a *timbale,* and cover them with the following preparation: rub half-pound of wild strawberries through a sieve; add a little raspberry sauce to the *purée,* that it may acquire a pink tint; and then add the same quantity of very stiff vanilla-flavored whipped cream.

Thoroughly cool these strawberries before serving them.

2684—CARDINAL STRAWBERRIES   *Fraises Cardinal*

Set some fine, cooled strawberries in a *timbale;* coat them with raspberry sauce, or a *purée* of fresh raspberries, and sprinkle the latter with slivered fresh almonds.

2685—ZELMA KUNTZ STRAWBERRIES   *Fraises Zelma Kuntz*

Put some fine, cooled strawberries in a *timbale.* Cover them with a raspberry *purée,* combined with an equal quantity of whipped cream.

Decorate, by means of the pastry-bag, with whipped cream, and sprinkle with a crushed *pralin* of filberts.

GOOSEBERRIES (GROSEILLES VERTES)

2686—GOOSEBERRY FOOL   *Gooseberry-fool*

Poach one pound of green gooseberries in some thin syrup. When they are cooked, drain them thoroughly; rub them through a sieve, and collect the *purée* in a flat saucepan.

Work this *purée* on ice, and add the necessary amount of icing sugar to it.

The amount of the icing sugar varies according to the acidity of the fruit and the sweetness of the *poaching*-syrup.

Combine with the *purée* an equal quantity of very stiffly whipped cream; set the preparation in the shape of a dome in a *timbale;* decorate its surface, by means of a pastry-bag, with whipped cream, and serve very cold.

TANGERINES (MANDARINES)

2687—ALMINA TANGERINES   *Mandarines Almina*

Cut a slice of the peel from the stem-end of the tangerines by means of a round, even cutter, one inch in diameter. Then empty them, and fill the peels with a preparation of Bavarian cream with violets, combined with crumbled lady-fingers, sprinkled with Maraschino. Close the tangerines with the slice cut off at the start; let them set in a cool place, and, at the last moment, lay them on a dish covered with a folded napkin.

2688—TANGERINES WITH CREAM   *Mandarines à la Crème*

Empty the tangerines, and fill their peels with a somewhat thick tangerine Bavarian cream preparation, combined with a third of its bulk of fresh, raw cream.

Place them in ice until they have to be served; serve them as directed in the preceding recipe.

2689—SURPRISE TANGERINES   *Mandarines en Surprise*

Proceed as for the oranges, but for the orange ice substitute tangerine jelly.

2690—ORANGES WITH BLANC-MANGE　　　　*Oranges au Blanc-Manger*

Cut the oranges and empty them as directed in the case of tangerines. Then fill them with French blanc-mange (2625), and let it set. Close the oranges with the slices cut off at the start, and serve them on a napkin.

2691—RUBANEES ORANGES　　　　　　　*Oranges Rubanées*

Fill the empty orange-shells with regular layers of variously colored and flavored blanc-manges, or with alternated fruit jellies. When about to serve, quarter the oranges.

N.B.—These quartered oranges are sometimes used for the garnishing of cold desserts.

2692—SURPRISE ORANGES　　　　　　　*Oranges en Surprise*

Cut a slice across each orange, representing about one-fourth of their height, and scoop them out. Fill the shells with orange ice; cover the latter with Italian *meringue* (2383); fill the shells with cracked ice, lying on a tray, and set them in a sufficiently hot oven, to quickly brown the *meringue*. On taking the oranges out of the oven, close each with the slices cut from tnem at the start, in which are stuck imitation leaves and stalks, made from pulled sugar. Serve them on a napkin.

2693—SURPRISE SOUFFLE OF ORANGES

Oranges Soufflées en Surprise

Empty the oranges as above; garnish the rinds with an orange *soufflé* preparation, and cook the latter.

On taking the oranges out of the oven, cover the *soufflé* with the slices cut off at the start; set the oranges on a napkin, and serve them instantly.

PEACHES AND NECTARINES (PÊCHES ET NECTARINES)

As nectarines may be prepared after the same recipes as peaches, there is no need to give special recipes for the former.

2694—AIGLON PEACHES　　　　　　　　*Pêches Aiglon*

After having peeled the peaches, *poach* them in a vanilla-flavored syrup, and leave them to cool. Drain them, serve them upon a layer of vanilla ice-cream, spread in a false-bottomed silver *timbale,* the inner compartment of which contains cracked ice. Sprinkle crystallized violets over the peaches; set the *timbale* in a block of ice, carved to represent an eagle, and cover the whole with a veil of spun sugar.

2695—AURORA PEACHES *Pêches à l'Aurore*

Poach the peeled peaches in a Kirsch-flavored syrup, and let them cool there. Drain them; set them in a silver *timbale,* upon a layer of "iced *mousse* with strawberries" (2917), and coat the whole with a Curaçao-flavored *sabayon.*

2696—ALEXANDRA PEACHES *Pêches Alexandra*

Poach the peaches in a vanilla-flavored syrup and let them cool completely. Set them in a *timbale* surrounded by ice containing on its bottom a layer of vanilla ice-cream, covered with a strawberry *purée.* Sprinkle the peaches with white and red rose-petals, and veil the whole with spun sugar.

2697—CARDINAL PEACHES *Pêches Cardinal*

Poach the peaches in vanilla-flavored syrup, and, when they are quite cold, serve them in a *timbale.* Cover them with a very red, sweetened, raspberry *purée,* flavored with Kirsch, and sprinkled with very white, slithered fresh almonds.

2698—DAME-BLANCHE PEACHES *Pêches Dame-Blanche*

Poach the peaches in vanilla-flavored syrup. When they are cold, set them in a *timbale* upon a layer of vanilla ice-cream, covered with thin slices of pineapple steeped in Maraschino and Kirsch.

Between each peach, and in every crevice, pipe some balls of whipped cream, laid by means of a pastry-bag, fitted with a fancy tube.

2699—MELBA PEACHES *Pêches Melba*

Poach the peaches in vanilla-flavored syrup. Put them in a *timbale* upon a layer of vanilla ice-cream, and coat them with a raspberry *purée.*

2700—PETIT-DUC PEACHES *Pêches Petit-Duc*

Prepare the peaches as under (2698), but use small heaps of red-currant jelly instead of rosettes of cream.

2701—SULTANA PEACHES   *Pêches Sultan₁*

Poach the peaches in vanilla-flavored syrup, and let them cool.

Set them in a *timbale* upon a layer of pistachio ice, and coat them with very cold, thickened syrup, flavored with rose *essence*.

Veil the whole with spun sugar, and set the *timbale* in a block of ice.

2702—CHATEAU-LAFITTE PEACHES   *Pêches Château-Lafitte*

Scald the peaches; peel them, and cut them in half.

Poach them in sufficient Château-Laffite wine to cover them, and sugar the wine to the extent of ten oz. of sugar per bottle of wine.

Leave them to cool in the syrup, and put them in a silver *timbale*.

Reduce the wine by three-quarters; thicken it with a little raspberry-flavored, red-currant jelly.

When this syrup is quite cold, sprinkle the peaches with it.

2703—IMPERATRICE PEACHES   *Pêches à l'Impératrice*

Cut the peaches in half; *poach* them in a vanilla-flavored syrup, and let them cool. Then drain and dry them; fill the cut side of each of the half-peaches with enough vanilla ice-cream to give them the appearance of whole fruit. Coat the peach-side of each with some stiff apricot sauce, and roll them in *pralined* slivered almonds.

Serve these peaches upon a cushion of *Génoise,* saturated with Kirsch and Maraschino, set upon a dry-paste base, and *glazed* with raspberry *glaze.*

Veil the whole with spun sugar.

2704—ROSE-CHERI PEACHES   *Pêches Rose-Chéri*

Poach the peaches in vanilla-flavored syrup, and let them cool. Put them in a *timbale;* cover them with a *purée* of pineapple with finest champagne, and serve very cold.

2705—ROSE-POMPOM PEACHES   *Pêches Rose-Pompom*

Scald and peel some fine peaches; *poach* them in vanilla-flavored syrup, and let them cool. Stone them without opening or breaking them too much, and in the place of the stone, put some very firm vanilla ice-cream.

Set these reconstructed peaches in a silver *timbale,* upon a layer of raspberry ice; cover them with *pralined* whipped cream; and before serving put them for thirty minutes in the refrigerator.

At the last moment, veil the *timbale* with pink, spun sugar.

PEARS (POIRES)

2706—ALMA PEARS   *Poires Alma*

Peel the pears and *poach* them in a syrup made from one quart of water, one-half pint of port wine, eight ounces of sugar, and the *blanched* and chopped *zest* of an orange. Cool: set them in a *timbale;* sprinkle them with powdered *pralin,* and serve a whipped cream at the same time.

2707—CARDINAL PEARS   *Poires Cardinal*

Poach the pears in a vanilla-flavored syrup, and then proceed as directed under (2697).

2708—CARIGNAN PEARS   *Poires à la Carignan*

Evenly peel some very fine dessert pears, and cook them in a vanilla-flavored syrup; keeping them fairly firm. Drain them on a dish and let them cool. This done, trim them flat at their base, and scoop them from underneath by means of a sharp spoon, after having outlined the circumference of the opening with a plain sharp knife.

Fill them with a preparation of "Bombe au chocolat praliné" (2826).

Close the pears with a little round of *Génoise,* stamped out with the same cutter as that used for the pears.

Set them on a tray; coat them speedily with apricot jam cooked to the *small-thread* stage (215° F.); *glaze* them with chocolate *fondant,* and keep them for three hours in a very cold refrigerator. Meanwhile, prepare as many small *Génoise* squares as there are pears; and make them one-quarter inch wider than the diameter of the pears. Saturate these square bases with Anisette, and by means of a little apricot jam cooked to the *small-thread* stage (215° F.), stick each of them on to very thin, dry-paste bases of the same size. Coat these prepared bases with the same apricot jam, and garnish them all round, as also their uncovered corners, with *pralined* slivered almonds.

When about to serve, take the pears out of the refrigerator, set them on these bases: stick into each a stalk and a leaf, made from pulled sugar; and serve on a napkin.

N.B.—Each pear should be cut vertically into two, three, or four pieces, subject to its size.

2709—FELICIA PEARS   *Poires Félicia*

Poach some quartered bartlett pears in vanilla-flavored syrup and
let them cool. Cook also, in a pink syrup, some very small halved
pears.

Arrange the quarters in the middle of a border of Viennese cream
(2641) laid out upon a dish. Cover them with a pyramid of vanilla-
flavored whipped cream, and sprinkle its surface with crushed, red
pralines.

Surround the cream border with the pink half-pears.

2710—FLORENTINE PEARS   *Poires à la Florentine*

Fill an oiled ring-mould with a semolina Bavarian cream preparation, and let it set. Turn it out at the last moment, and fill the
middle of the border with stewed pears, set on by means of a
vanilla-flavored apricot *purée*.

2711—HELENE PEARS   *Poires Hélène*

Poach the pears in vanilla-flavored syrup and let them cool.

When about to serve, set them in a *timbale* upon a layer of vanilla
ice-cream, sprinkled with crystallized violets.

Serve a hot, chocolate sauce separately.

2712—MARQUISE PEARS   *Poires Marquise*

Cook the pears in a vanilla-flavored syrup, and drain them that
they may cool. This done, coat them again and again with some very
stiff raspberry-flavored red-currant jelly, and sprinkle them instantly with chopped, burnt almonds.

Set the pears on a "Diplomat Pudding" (2660), made in a *manqué
mould*, and turned out on a round dish. Surround the base of
the pudding with a border of apple-jelly *croûtons*, neatly cut to
triangular shapes.

2713—MARY GARDEN PEARS   *Poires Mary Garden*

Cook the pears in syrup; cool them, and put them in a *timbale*,
upon a raspberry sauce, combined with half-sugared cherries softened in tepid water for a few minutes.

Decorate the pears with whipped cream.

2714—MELBA PEARS   *Poires Melba*

Poach the pears in a vanilla-flavored syrup, and proceed as di
rected under (2699).

2715—PRALINED PEARS   *Poires Pralinées*

Stew the pears and let them cool. Set them in a *timbale,* and coat with some *frangipan* cream, thinned by means of a little raw cream.

Between each pear, set a well-moulded tablespoon of whipped cream, and cover the whole with *chopped*-almond *pralin.*

Serve a cold or hot chocolate sauce at the same time.

2716—PEARS A LA RELIGIEUSE   *Poires à la Religieuse*

Stew the pears in a vanilla-flavored syrup; cool them, and serve them in a shallow porcelain *timbale* equal in depth to the length of the pears.

Cover them with a somewhat thin chocolate Bavarois preparation, and place the whole for two hours in the refrigerator before serving.

2717—PEARS WITH RUM   *Poires au Rhum*

Stew the pears and set them in a *timbale.*

Thicken the syrup with arrowroot or cornstarch, color it faintly with pink; flavor it with rum; pour it over the pears, and let them cool.

N.B.—These pears may also be served hot, after the same recipe; except that the rum is poured over the pears, hot, at the last moment, and lighted at the table.

2718—QUEEN EMMA PEARS   *Poires à la Reine Emma*

Mould a Flamri preparation (2649) in an even ring-mould, decorated with candied fruit. Set this to *poach,* and, when it is cold, turn it out on a round dish.

In the middle set a pyramid of quartered pears, stewed in a vanilla-flavored syrup; coat the quarters with *frangipan* (2399) cream, combined with a quarter of its bulk of crushed, dry macaroons, and with double its volume of very stiff whipped cream.

Decorate the top, by means of a pastry-bag, with whipped cream; and serve some Kirsch-flavored apricot sauce separately.

APPLES

2719—ROYALE APPLES   *Pommes à la Royale*

Peel some small apples, core them by means of a corer, and *poach* them in vanilla-flavored syrup. When they are quite cold, coat them with red-currant jelly, and arrange them in a circle, each upon a *tartlet* of blanc-mange. Fill their midst with chopped Maraschino jelly.

VARIOUS COLD SWEETS (ENTREMETS)

2720—SPONGE CAKE A LA REINE　　　　　*Biscuit à la Reine*

Cook, in a *manqué mould,* a Savoy-biscuit preparation (2439), and let it cool.

With a little apricot jam, cooked to the *small-thread* stage (215° F.), stick this biscuit on a dry-paste base; saturate it with cold syrup, flavored with Kümmel, and by means of a pastry-bag decorate it all round and on its edges with royale icing.

Turn out upon it a Bavarian cream with Maraschino, moulded in a *Richelieu mould* of proportionate size.

2721—MEXICAINE CRUST　　　　　*Croûte à la Mexicaine*

Cut some slices three inches long by one-third inch thick from a stale *Génoise.* Coat them with a Condé *pralin* (2352), and dry them in a moderate oven.

Set these crusts in a crown on a round dish, and garnish their midst with a rocky pyramid of Plombière ice (2614), projecting above them.

2722—DIPLOMATE WITH FRUITS　　　　　*Diplomate aux Fruits*

Prepare a base of *Génoise* with fruit, *glazed* with apricot jam, cooked to the *small-thread* stage (215° F.); a Bavarois with fruits.

Turn out the latter upon the former, and surround the whole with stewed fruit of the same kind as those used for the Bavarian cream.

2723—FLOATING ISLAND　　　　　*Ile Flottante*

Take a stale Savoy biscuit (2349), and cut it into thin slices.

Saturate it with Kirsch and Maraschino, coat them with apricot jam, and sprinkle the latter with currants and chopped almonds. Put the slices one upon the other, in such a way as to reconstruct the biscuit, and coat the whole with a layer of sweetened and vanilla-flavored whipped cream.

Sprinkle the cream with slithered pistachios and currants; set the whole on a long shallow compote dish, and surround it with vanilla-flavored English custard (2398), or raspberry syrup.

2724—MILK JUNKET *Junket-Milk*

Gently heat one quart of milk. When it has reached 95° F. take it off the fire; add two and one-half oz. of sugar to it; flavor it as fancy may suggest; put into it six drops of russet-apple *essence* (or two pastils of russet-apple *essence,* dissolved in six drops of water); pour it into a *timbale,* and serve it very cold.

N.B.—This very delicate and simple dessert is little else, indeed, than flavored and sweetened milk, caused to set by the combined agencies of heat and russet-apple *essence,* nowadays accomplished with Rennet.

2725—MACEDOINE OF COOLED FRUITS

Macédoine de Fruits Rafraîchis

Take some fresh fruit of the season, such as ripe Bartlett pears and peaches, peeled and sliced apricots and bananas, and add to it some small or large strawberries, raspberries, white- and red-currants; skinned, fresh almonds, etc.

Set these fruits in a *timbale* surrounded by ice, mixing them well together; sprinkle them with a syrup at 30° (saccharom.), flavored with Kirsch or Maraschino, and let them steep for an hour or two; taking care to toss them from time to time.

2726—EUGENIA-ITALIAN CREAM *Eugénia-Crème à l'Italienne*

Select some very ripe Eugenia or Rose apples; peel, slice, and set to steep in a bowl, with Maraschino-flavored syrup.

Set the fruit in a *timbale,* upon a layer of vanilla ice-cream; decorate them on top with whipped cream, and sprinkle the latter with crystallized violets.

2727—MARQUISE ALICE *Marquise Alice*

Prepare a *pralin-*flavored Bavarian cream in a *manqué mould:* garnish the inside with sponge lady fingers, saturated with Anisette.

Turn it out on a dish, and completely cover it with an even coat of very stiff, sweetened and vanilla-flavored whipped cream.

On top, lay some parallel lines of red-currant jelly, by means of the pastry-bag; and then cut these lines at right angles, with the point of a small knife. Surround the base with small puff-paste triangles, coated with *Pralin,* dried in the oven.

2728—ORIENTALE MELON *Melon à l'Orientale*

Take a melon that is just ripe; make a circular incision round its stalk, and remove the bung. Seed and scoop out the flesh by means of a silver spoon and cut in dice.

Copiously sprinkle the inside of the melon with icing-sugar and fill it up with wild strawberries and the melon dice, spread in alternate layers, sprinkled with sugar. Complete with one-sixth pint of Kirsch; close the melon with the bung, seal the joint with a thread of butter, and keep the melon in a cool place for two hours.

Place it on a napkin, and serve *gaufrettes* (thin wafers) at the same time.

2729—MELON FRAPPE   *Melon Frappé*

Select two very ripe, medium-sized melons, and, with the entire flesh of one of them, cleared of all the rind and seeds and rubbed through a fine sieve, prepare a *Granité* after (2930).

Cut the other melon round the stalk and open it. Completely remove the seeds; and, by means of a silver spoon, scoop out the flesh pieces, and set it to steep on ice with a little sugar and one of the following wines or liqueurs: Port, Curaçao, Rum, Kirsch or Maraschino.

Keep the emptied shell for thirty minutes in a refrigerator.

When about to serve, set the emptied melon on a small block of fancifully carved ice, and fill it up with the *Granité* and the steeped pulp spread in alternate layers. When the melon is full, return the bung to its place.

N.B.—This melon is served, by means of a spoon, upon iced plates, and it often takes the place of ices at the end of a dinner.

2730—SURPRISE MELON   *Melon en Surprise*

Empty the melon as above, and fill it with a *macédoine* of fresh fruits, combined with the scooped flesh of the melon, cut into dice and mixed with a sugared and Kirsch-flavored *purée* of wild strawberries.

Close the melon and keep it in the refrigerator for two hours.

2731—GARNISHED MERINGUES   *Meringués Garnies*

Join the *meringue* shells together in pairs, by means of some stiff sugared and flavored whipped cream or with some sort of ice, and serve them on a napkin.

2732—MONT-BLANC WITH STRAWBERRIES   *Mont-Blanc aux Fraises*

Add some small wild strawberries steeped in cold, vanilla-flavored syrup and drained, to some very stiff whipped cream; the proportions being four oz. of the former per quart of the latter.

Arrange in the shape of a dome; surround the base with large strawberries, rolled in beaten egg-whites and then in coarse crystallized sugar, and decorate the surface with large and very red halved-strawberries.

2733—MONT-BLANC WITH CHESTNUTS   *Mont-Blanc aux Marrons*

Cook some chestnuts in sweetened and vanilla-flavored milk and rub them through a sieve, over a ring mould; in order that the chestnut *purée,* falling in the form of vermicelli, may garnish the mould naturally.

Fill up the mould with the *purée* that has fallen over the sides of the mould; turn out the ring on a dish, and in the midst set an irregular and jagged mound of sugared and vanilla-flavored whipped cream.

2734—MONT-ROSE   *Mont-Rose*

Prepare a *Charlotte,* Plombière in a shallow *Madeleine* ice-mould.

Having turned out the Charlotte on a dish, cover it on top with tablespoons of whipped cream, combined with a *purée* of fresh raspberries, and so shaped as to imitate a pyramidic rock.

2735—EGGS IN SNOW (A LA NEIGE)   *Oeufs à la Neige*

Mould some ordinary *meringue,* by means of a spoon, to represent eggs; and drop the mouldings into a saucepan containing some boiling sugared and vanilla-flavored milk. Turn the *meringues* over in the milk, that they may *poach* evenly, and, as soon as they are firm, drain them in a sieve.

Strain the milk through muslin; add six egg yolks, and with it prepare an English custard (2398).

Set the egg-shaped *meringues* on a large shallow compote dish and cover them with the prepared custard, kept very cold.

2736—MOULDED EGGS IN SNOW (A LA NEIGE)

Oeufs à la Neige Moulés

Prepare the *meringues* and the English custard as above; but to the latter add about five ounces gelatine leaves soaked in cold water. Set the egg-shaped *meringues* in an oiled border-mould; cover them with the very cold custard, which, however, should not have set; and let the preparation set in the cool, or surrounded by ice.

2737—REJANE MOUSSELINE OF EGGS   *Mousseline d'Oeufs Réjane*

By means of a pastry-bag, fitted with a plain tube, lay some ordinary *meringues* upon sheets of white paper, in shapes resembling large macaroons.

Slip the sheets of paper into boiling, sugared and vanilla-flavored milk, and pull out the sheets of paper as soon as the *meringues* slip off. Complete the *poaching* of the *meringues,* and drain them.

Set these *meringues,* two by two, in silver or porcelain egg-dishes; place a fine, *poached* half apricot in the middle of each, and cover the whole with a few teaspoons of English custard.

2738—MIMI MOUSSELINE OF EGGS   *Mousseline d'Oeufs Mimi*

This is a preparation of ordinary Italian *meringue* (2383), *poached* in a *bain-marie* (water-bath), in a caramel-coated mould. Let the contents get quite cold before turning out, and serve some stewed, fresh fruit and an English custard (2398) separately.

2739—IMPERATRICE RICE   *Riz à l'Impératrice*

Make a vanilla-flavored preparation of rice for desserts, using the quantities of milk and sugar already prescribed. When the rice is cooked, and somewhat cold, add to it four oz. of a *salpicon* of candied fruit and four tablespoons of apricot jam, per one-half lb. of raw rice. Then combine with it an equal quantity of Kirsch-flavored Bavarian preparation, or one pint of thick English custard and one pint of whipped cream.

Let a layer of red-currant jelly set upon the bottom of a Bavarian cream mould; then pour the above preparation into the latter and let the whole set, either in a cool place or surrounded by ice.

When about to serve, turn out on a napkin.

2740—MALTESE RICE   *Riz à la Maltaise*

Prepare the rice with milk as above, but flavor it with orange rind, and omit the apricot jam and the candied fruit *salpicon*. Combine with it an equal quantity of orange Bavarian cream preparation; pour the whole into a *dome-mould,* and let it set on ice. When about to serve, turn out upon a round dish, and cover it with alternate rows of orange-sections, skinned and steeped in a syrup flavored with orange-rind.

2741—SUEDOISE OF FRUITS   *Suédoise de Fruits*

As I mentioned in my remarks upon the preparation of jellies, a Suédoise of fruit is a jelly moulded in an *aspic mould* and garnished with layers of stewed fruit, the colors and kinds of which should be contrasted as much as possible.

2742—FRAISALIA TIMBALE   *Timbale Fraisalia*

Prepare a *timbale* of Savarin paste (2371) in a *Charlotte mould.*
When it is baked and cooled, remove the crumbs from its inside
leaving a thickness of half an inch on its bottom and sides; coat
it thinly with Kirsch-flavored syrup, and return the *timbale* to the
mould.

Now garnish it with alternate layers of vanilla-flavored, Bavarian
cream preparation and wild strawberries, steeped in Kirsch. Let
it set in a cool place, or surround the mould with ice. Turn out
the *timbale* first upon a plate; overturn it on a dish, and upon it
set a pyramid of vanilla-flavored whipped cream. *Stud* the latter
all over with small, very red strawberries, or garnish it with large
halved-strawberries.

Surround the *timbale* with fine dice of strawberry jelly.

2743—TIVOLI WITH STRAWBERRIES   *Tivoli aux Fraises*

Coat an ornamented mould, fitted with a central tube, with a
thick coat of very clear, Kirsch-flavored jelly. Fill the mould with
a Bavarian cream preparation, combined with plenty of wild
strawberry *purée,* and let its contents set. Turn it out, when about
to serve, and surround it with very clear, chopped Kirsch-flavored
jelly.

CHAPTER II

ICES

Ices, with their accompanying "petits fours," bring the dinner to a close—at least as far as Cookery is concerned; and, when they are well prepared and daintily dished, they are the consummation of all that is delicate and good. In no other department of the work has the culinary artist so freely indulged his fancy, or created such delectable tid-bits; and, though Italy be the cradle of the ice-worker's art, though the Neapolitans have deservedly maintained their reputation as authorities in this matter, to French chefs, certainly, is due the credit of those innovations which have perfected this important branch of dietetic science.

2744—THE MAKING OF ICES   *La Préparation des Glaces*

Whatever be the kind of ices required, they should always be prepared in advance; for none of these preparations can be made ready at a moment's notice.

There are two distinct operations in the confection of ices:—

(1) The making of the preparation.

(2) The freezing and the moulding of the preparation. I shall begin by dealing with the second operation, which remains the same for all ices, and is the essential part of the procedure.

To freeze an ice preparation is to surround it with cracked ice, mixed with sodium chloride (sea-salt or freezing salt) and saltpetre. The action of these two salts upon the ice causes a considerable drop in the temperature, which speedily congeals any enclosed liquid. Subject to their nature, ices are either moulded and frozen directly in their moulds, like the light ices: iced Biscuits, iced *Soufflés,* Puddings, *Mousses,* Parfaits, Bombes, etc.; or first frozen in a special utensil called a freezer, and then moulded and frozen again. Cream and syrup ices are prepared by the second method; and this I shall now describe.

The freezers, in which the freezing takes place, are generally

wielded by hand, either directly or by means of some mechanism.
They should be of pure tin, and fitted at their base on to a central
pivot which turns in a socket, fixed in the wooden case which holds
the freezer.

Having hermetically closed the latter, surround it with cracked
ice containing three lbs. of salt and eight oz. of saltpetre per
twenty-five lbs.

The freezer should be one-third of its height out of the ice, in
order that no particle of salted ice may accidently fall into the
preparation while it is being frozen. The ice should be snugly
massed, by means of a special pestle, round the freezer. This
operation constitutes the packing, and should be done at least ten
minutes in advance if possible.

Having thus prepared the freezer, pour into it the preparation
to be frozen and then either keep it in motion by rocking the
utensil to and fro, by grasping the handle on the cover (if the
apparatus is worked by hand), or by turning the handle if the
utensil is on a central axle, fitted with the usual mechanism. In
either case, the rotary movement of the utensil causes the preparation to splash continually against the sides of the freezer, where it
rapidly congeals and the congealed portions are removed by means
of a special paddle, as quickly as they form, until the whole becomes
a smooth and a completely frozen mass. The delicacy and creaminess
of the ice depend a great deal upon the care with which this freezing
operation is effected; hence the preference which is now given to
freezers fitted with a mechanism whereby two fans revolve inside in
a direction opposite to that of the body of the machine, and thus
not only detach the congealed portions of the preparation under
treatment from the sides of the receptacle, but also work it with
a regularity impossible to human motion.

2745—THE MOULDING OF ICES   *Le Moulage des Glaces*

Having thus frozen the preparation, it may now be set in rock-
form on a napkin, as it used sometimes to be served in the past,
or in glasses. But as a rule it is put into special moulds, having
closely-fitting covers. These moulds should be carefully filled, and
banged out on a folded napkin, that the ice may settle and drive
out any air which might cause holes being found in the preparation. When it is filled, place the mould in a receptacle of a suitable
size, and surround it with cracked ice, prepared as for the packing.
The mould should remain at least an hour in the ice, in the case

of an ordinary ice, and an extra two hours if the ice be light and not previously frozen as are the Bombes.

When about to serve, take the mould out of the ice; wash it to rid it of the taint of salt; dip it in tepid water for an instant, that the surface of the preparation inside may melt and separate easily from the mould. Overturn the mould; and turn out the ice upon a folded napkin lying on a dish.

2746—PREPARATIONS FOR SIMPLE ICES

Compositions pour Glaces Simples

Preparations for simple ices are of two kinds: those made from cream, and those made from syrup; the latter being principally used for fruit ices.

As the quantities of sugar and eggs used for these preparations vary exceedingly, the following recipes have been based upon a working average.

If creamier ices be required, all that is needed is an increase in the sugar and egg-yolks per quart of milk; while, if the ices be required harder but less creamy, the two ingredients above mentioned should be proportionately reduced.

As an example of the difference that may exist between cream preparations, I might instance the case of ice-cream, which may be made from seven to sixteen egg-yolks, and six oz. to one lb. of sugar per quart of milk. In regard to ices made from syrups and fruit, their preparations may measure from 15° to 30° or 32° (saccharometer) respectively.

(The use of the saccharometer for gauging the sugar content of syrups is still in use today by the manufacturers and probably by chefs in large establishments. In only a few dessert recipes are directions given for measuring the sugar mixture by degrees. If the reader, inspired by the combinations and the wonderful flavors the recipes suggest, wishes to use such an instrument he may put the instructions to profitable use by measuring with a Brix Hydrometer, which takes the place of a saccharometer.

The hydrometer is plunged into a hydrometer jar filled with syrup. The syrup must be 68 degrees Fahrenheit, since the instrument is regulated to measure at this temperature. According to the density of the sugar content, the hydrometer will sink into the syrup. The reading on the graduated scale indicates the amount of sugar in the syrup.

A Brix Hydrometer may be purchased in many stores and

through the Taylor Instrument Companies of Rochester, New York. They sell for a little more than two dollars.—Ed.)

2747—ICE CREAM PREPARATION (General Recipe)

Composition pour Glace-Crème

Work two-thirds lb. of sugar and ten egg-yolks in a saucepan until the mixture reaches the ribbon-stage (2376). Dilute it, little by little, with one quart of boiling milk, and stir over a moderate fire until the preparation coats the withdrawn spoon. Avoid boiling, as it might separate the custard.

Strain the whole into a basin and stir it from time to time until it is quite cold.

N.B.—For the various ice cream preparations, the amount of sugar and number of egg-yolks, as also the procedure, do not change. They are only distinguishable by the particular flavor or infusion which may happen to characterize them.

VARIOUS ICE CREAM PREPARATIONS

2748—ALMOND ICE CREAM   *Glace-Crème aux Amandes*

Finely pound three and a half oz. of freshly-skinned sweet almonds and five bitter almonds; adding to them, little by little, in order to facilitate the pounding, a few tablespoons of water.

Set this almond paste to steep, twenty minutes beforehand, in the boiling milk, and prepare the cream as directed above, with the same quantities of sugar and egg-yolks.

2749—ASPARAGUS ICE CREAM   *Glace-Crème aux Asperges*

Parboil six oz. of asparagus tips for two minutes. Thoroughly drain them; quickly pound them, together with a few tablespoons of milk, and set this asparagus paste to steep in the boiled milk.

2750—FILBERT ICE CREAM   *Glace-Crème aux Avelines*

Slightly grill three and half oz. of filberts; finely pound them, together with a few tablespoons of milk, and set this paste to steep for twenty minutes in the boiled milk.

2751—COFFEE ICE CREAM   *Glace-Crème au Café*

Add two oz. of freshly-grilled and crushed coffee beans to the boiled milk, and let them steep for twenty minutes.

Or, with an equivalent amount of ground coffee and half a pint of water, prepare a very strong infusion and add it to one and a half pints of boiled milk.

2752—CHOCOLATE ICE CREAM   *Glace-Crème au Chocolat*

Dissolve eight oz. of grated chocolate in half pint of water, and add one quart of boiled milk, in which a large stick of vanilla has previously been steeped. For this preparation, eight oz. of sugar and seven egg-yolks will be found sufficient, if the chocolate used be sweet.

2753—WALNUT ICE CREAM   *Glace-Crème aux Noix*

Finely pound three and a half oz. of well-peeled walnut meats with a few tablespoons of water, and set them to steep for twenty minutes in boiling milk.

2754—PISTACHIO ICE CREAM   *Glace-Crème aux Pistaches*

Pound two oz. of sweet almonds, and two and a half oz. of freshly-peeled pistachios; moistening them with a few drops of milk. Set the paste to steep for twenty minutes in the boiled milk.

2755—PRALINE ICE CREAM   *Glace-Crème au Pralin*

Pound and rub through a sieve four oz. of almond *pralin,* and add one quart of previously-prepared vanilla-flavored custard.

2756—TEA ICE CREAM   *Glace-Crème au Thé*

Add one pint of very strong tea to one and a half pints of boiled milk, and make the preparation in the usual way.

2757—VANILLA ICE CREAM   *Glace-Crème à la Vanille*

When the milk has boiled, steep in it one large stick of vanilla for twenty minutes.

N.B.—If these various preparations be required more creamy, the milk may be wholly or partly replaced by fresh cream. Also when the preparation is congealed, it may be combined with one-sixth pint of whipped cream per quart.

2758—PREPARATIONS FOR FRUIT ICES

Compositions pour Glaces aux Fruits

The base of these preparations is a syrup of sugar at 32° (saccharom.), to which a *purée* of fruit, a flavoring, or a liqueur is added, which will give the ice its character. All these preparations require lemon juice, the quantity of which varies according to the acidity of the fruit used, but which, even in the case of the tartest fruits, should not measure less than the amount that may be extracted from a whole lemon per quart of the preparation.

Orange juice may also be used, more especially for red-fruit ices; while the juices of the orange and the lemons combined throw the flavor of the fruit under treatment into remarkable relief.

In the season the juices are extracted from fresh fruit, pressed and rubbed through a fine sieve. When the season is over the preserved juice of fruit is used.

All red-fruit ices are improved, once they are set, by an addition of half pint of raw, fresh cream per quart of the preparation.

2759—THE MAKING OF FRUIT ICE PREPARATIONS
Pour Faire les Preparations pour Glaces aux Fruits

These preparations are made in two ways as follows:—

Rub the fruit through a fine sieve, after having pounded it if its nature permit. Dilute the *purée* with an equal quantity of cold sugar syrup at 32° (saccharom.), and add lemon juice in a quantity subject to the acidity of the treated fruit.

This mixture of ingredients should always be cold, and should be tested with saccharom. (pèse-sirops). If the instrument marks more than the proper degree, dilute the preparation with a little water; if it marks less, add syrup until the required degree is reached.

Or pound the fruit with an average quantity of ten oz. of sugar per lb.; but remember that this proportion may be modified either way, subject to the sweetness of the fruit used.

Rub the whole through a sieve; and then, to obtain the proper degree of strength, add the necessary quantity of filtered water.

2760—LIQUEUR ICE PREPARATIONS
Compositions pour Glaces aux Liqueurs

These preparations are made by adding to the syrup or the cream which forms the base of the ice a given quantity of the selected liqueur, the latter being generally added when the preparation is cold.

The proportion of one-fifth pint of liqueur per quart of syrup may be taken as an average. Subject to the requirements this liqueur flavor may be intensified with strong tea for rum ices; with orange-rind for Curaçao-flavored ices, with fresh, crushed cherry-stones for Kirsch ices, etc.

These preparations should always contain some lemon-juice, and their strength should reach the average degree indicated for fruit ices.

Various Fruit-Ice Preparations

2761—APRICOT ICE *Glace à l'Abricot*

Take one pint of fresh apricot *purée,* one pint of syrup, and the juice of two lemons. The strength of the preparation should measure 18° or 19° (saccharometer).

2762—PINEAPPLE ICE *Glace à l'Ananas*

Set to steep for two hours one pint of grated or pounded pineapple in one pint of syrup. Rub the whole through a sieve, add the juice of one lemon and a few drops of Kirsch, and test the preparation, which should measure from 18° to 20°.

2763—BANANA ICE *Glace aux Bananes*

Set one pint of pounded banana pulp to steep for two hours in one pint of Maraschino-flavored syrup. Add the juice of three lemons, and rub through a sieve. This preparation should measure from 20° to 21°.

2764—CHERRY ICE *Glace aux Cerises*

Crush one pint of pitted cherries, and pound their stones. Set the whole to steep for one hour in one pint of syrup, flavored with Kirsch. Rub through a sieve and add the juice of half a lemon. The preparation should measure 21°.

2765—LEMON ICE *Glace au Citron*

Set the *zests* of three lemon peels to steep for three hours in one pint of cold syrup. Add the juice of four lemons and of two oranges, and strain. The preparation should measure 22°.

2766—STRAWBERRY ICE *Glace aux Fraises*

Mix one pint of strawberry *purée* with one pint of syrup, and add the juice of two oranges and of two lemons. Or pound two lbs. of strawberries with one lb. of powdered sugar; add the juice of oranges and lemons as above; rub the whole through a sieve, and add the necessary amount of filtered water to bring the preparation to 16° or 18°.

2767—RASPBERRY ICE *Glace aux Framboises*

Proceed as for (2766), and use the same quantities.

2768—RED-CURRANT ICE *Glace à la Groseille*

Mix one pint of red-currant juice with one pint of syrup. In view of the natural acidity of the fruit, lemon-juice may be dispensed with. The preparation should measure 20°.

2769—TANGERINE ICE *Glace aux Mandarines*

Throw the *zests* of the rinds of four tangerines into one and one-half pints of boiling syrup. Let the whole cool; rub it through a sieve, and finish it with the juice of six tangerines, two oranges and one lemon. The preparation should measure 21°.

2770—MELON ICE *Glace au Melon*

Mix one pint of very ripe melon pulp with one pint of syrup, the juice of two oranges and one lemon, and one tablespoon of orange-flower water. Rub the whole through a sieve. The mixture should measure 22°.

2771—ORANGE ICE *Glace à l'Orange*

Throw the *zests* of the rinds of four oranges into one quart of boiling syrup. Let the whole cool; add the juice of four oranges and one lemon, and rub it through a sieve. It should measure 21°.

2772—PEACH ICE *Glace aux Pêches*

Proceed as for (2761), using wall peaches (those grown on a tree near a wall) if possible.

2773—PEAR ICE *Glace aux Poires*

Peel, core, and pound some fine Bartlett pears, with one lb. of powdered sugar per two-thirds lb. of the fruit; and add the juice of two lemons per lb. of pears. Rub the whole through a sieve, and add enough filtered water to bring it to 22°.

2774—PLUM ICE *Glace aux Prunes*

Proceed as for (2761), bringing the preparation to 20°.

2775—GRAPE ICE *Glace aux Raisins*

Add to one and one-half pints of the juice of sweet, pressed grapes the juice of three lemons and the necessary quantity of powdered sugar to bring the preparation to 20°. Rub the whole through a sieve.

2776—VIOLET ICE   *Glace aux Violettes*

Put half a lb. of cleaned violet petals into one and one-half pints of boiling syrup. Let them steep for ten minutes; strain the whole through a sieve; let it cool, and finish it with the juice of three lemons. The preparation should measure from 20° to 21°.

VARIOUS ICES

2777—ALHAMBRA ICE   *Glace Alhambra*

Take a *Madeleine-mould;* coat its bottom and sides with vanilla ice-cream and fill it with whipped cream, combined with fresh strawberries, steeped for two hours in Kümmel, which should afterwards be added to the whipped cream.

2778—CARMEN ICE   *Glace Carmen*

Take a fluted mould. Garnish it with vertical and alternate layers of raspberry ice, coffee ice, and vanilla ice-cream.

2779—COUNTESS MARIE ICE   *Glace Comtesse-Marie*

Take a special *square mould,* even or ornamented on the top. Coat it with strawberry ice; fill it with vanilla ice-cream; and, after turning it out, decorate it, with a pastry-bag (fitted with a fancy tube), with vanilla ice-cream.

2780—SUNSET ICE   *Glace Coucher de Soleil*

Select one pound of fine very ripe strawberries, and put them in a silver *timbale*. Sprinkle them with ten ounces of powdered sugar and one liqueur-glass of Grand-Marnier liqueur; cover the *timbale* and keep it on ice for half an hour.

Then rub the strawberries through a sieve; and, with their *purée,* make a preparation after the directions given under Fruit Ices. Freeze this preparation in the freezer, and, when it is set, combine with it one pint of whipped cream. Now cover the freezer; surround it again with ice if necessary, and keep it thus for thirty-five to forty minutes. This done, put the ice preparation with care in pyramid form in crystal bowls.

N.B.—This ice gets its name from its color, which should be that of the western sky during a fine sunset.

2781—DAME JEANNE ICE   *Glace Dame-Jeanne*

Take a *Madeleine-mould;* coat it with vanilla ice-cream, and fill it with whipped cream, combined with *pralined* orange flowers.

2782—DORA ICE   *Glace Dora*

Take a *Madeleine-mould;* coat it with vanilla ice-cream, and fill it with Kirsch-flavored whipped cream combined with pineapple dice and Bar red-currant jam.

2783—ETOILE DU BERGER ICE   *Glace Etoile de Berger*

Take a *star-shaped* mould, or a *Madeleine-mould* with a star on its bottom. Coat it with raspberry ice, and fill it with Benedictine flavored *Mousse.*

Turn it out upon a regular disc, consisting of a thick layer of white spun sugar, lying on a dish. This spun sugar throws the ice into relief, and emits rays which dart out from between the points of the star.

2784—FLEURETTE ICE   *Glace Fleurette*

Take a *square mould.* Garnish it with strawberry and pineapple ice, laid in very regular, superimposed layers. After turning it out decorate with lemon ice.

2785—FRANCILLON ICE   *Glace Francillon*

Take a *square mould;* coat it with coffee ice, and fill it with liqueur-brandy ice.

2786—FROMAGE ICES   *Glaces Fromages*

These ices are made in *fluted moulds,* and generally with two differently flavored and colored ices, set vertically in the mould.

2787—GOURMETS' ICE   *Glace des Gourmets*

Take a *"bombe"* mould. Coat it with *pralined,* vanilla ice-cream. Fill it with alternate layers of chestnut ice flavored with rum, and vanilla-flavored whipped cream. When the ice is turned out, roll it in *pralined* slivered almonds.

2788—MOULDED ICES   *Glaces Moulées*

These ices are made in large or small moulds.

The large ices are moulded in tin moulds, fitted with hinged covers, and ornamented with some design. The small ones, which are generally served at evening parties, or are used to garnish larger ices, are made in similar moulds, shaped like flowers, fruit, birds, leaf-sprays, etc.

Any ice preparation may be used for these ices; but, as a rule, the preparation should have something in keeping with the design of the mould used.

Small moulded ices may be kept packed until they are served.
They may also be turned out in advance and kept in the refrigerator.

2789—ICE "DES ILES"   *Glace des Iles*

Take a *Madeleine-mould;* coat it with vanilla ice-cream, and fill
it with pineapple ice.

2790—MADELEINE ICE   *Glace Madeleine*

Take a *Madeleine-mould.* Fill it with vanilla ice-cream, combined
with half its bulk of whipped cream and candied fruit steeped in
Kirsch.

2791—FROSTED TANGERINES   *Mandarines Givrées*

Cut the tangerines on top, with a round, even cutter, in such
a way as to remove a round slice of their peel with the stalk attached,
and two leaves clinging to it.

With the juice of the tangerines prepare some tangerine ice,
after the directions given under Fruit-ice Preparations. Fill the
tangerines with this ice; cover them with the slices removed at
the start; and, with a brush, sprinkle the rinds of the fruit with
water, and place them in a refrigerator.

As soon as the tangerines are coated with frost, serve them on
a napkin.

2792—ICED TANGERINES "AUX PERLES DES ALPES" (CHARTREUSE
CANDY BALLS)   *Mandarines Glacées aux Perles de Alpes*

Empty the tangerines as above, and garnish them inside with
tangerine *mousse,* with which *Chartreuse* bon-bons have been mixed.
Cover them, and frost them as directed above.

2793—MARIE THERESE ICE   *Glace Marie-Thérèse*

Take a *Madeleine-mould;* coat it with chocolate ice, and fill it
with vanilla-flavored whipped cream.

After turning out, decorate it with pineapple ice.

2794—ICED MERINGUES   *Meringues Glacées*

Fill some *meringue* shells with some kind of spoon-moulded ice,
and set them on a napkin.

Or, fill the shells more sparingly and join them together in pairs.

2795—PLOMBIERE ICE *Glace Plombière*

Take a *parfait mould*. Garnish it with vanilla-ice cream combined with candied fruit, steeped in Kirsch; spreading the preparation in alternate layers with apricot jam.

COUPES

We are now concerned with bowls filled, either with differently-flavored ices, or with ices combined with whipped cream or candied fruit. The bowls used for this purpose should be of crystal.

2796—COUPES D'ANTIGNY *Coupes d'Antigny*

Three-quarters fill the bowls with Alpine-strawberry ice, or, failing this, four-seasons strawberry ice, combined with very light and strongly-flavored raw cream. The two most perfect examples of this cream are the "Fleurette Normande," and that which in the South of France is called "Crème Niçoise," and which comes from Alpine pastures. (In the United States we have very fine rich cream from Jersey and Guernsey cows, and all cream is graded according to butter fat content. This recipe calls for a 24–30% cream.—Ed.)

Upon the ice of each bowl set a half-peach, *poached* in vanilla-flavored syrup; and veil the whole thinly with spun sugar.

2797—COUPES CLO-CLO *Coupes Clo-Clo*

Fill the bottom of the bowls with vanilla ice cream, combined with fragments of candied chestnuts, steeped in Maraschino. Set a candied chestnut in the middle of the ice, and surround it by means of a pastry-bag with a border of whipped cream, containing strawberry *purée*.

2798—COUPES DAME BLANCHE *Coupes Dame Blanche*

Three-quarters fill the bowls with almond-milk (2506) ice. Upon the ice in each bowl set an overturned half-peach, *poached* in vanilla-flavored syrup, the hollow of which should be filled with Bar redcurrant jam. Surround the peaches with a ribbon of lemon ice, laid by means of a pastry-bag.

2799—COUPES DENISE *Coupes Denise*

Fill the bowls with Mocha ice, and sprinkle the latter with sweets containing liqueur (preferably rum). Cover with whipped cream laid on by means of the spoon.

2800—COUPES EDNA MAY   *Coupes Edna May*

Fill the bottom of the bowls with vanilla ice-cream, and upon the latter set some very cold stewed cherries. Cover the latter with a cone of whipped cream, tinted pink by means of a fresh raspberry *purée*.

2801—COUPES ELIZABETH   *Coupes Elizabeth*

These coupes do not contain ice. They are filled with very cold stewed choice bigaroon (large) cherries, *poached* in a Kirsch- and cherry-brandy-flavored syrup. The fruit is covered with whipped cream which is laid on by means of a spoon, and sprinkled with powdered spices in which cinnamon should predominate.

2802—COUPES EMMA CALVE   *Coupes Emma Calve*

Fill the bottom of the bowls with *pralined* vanilla ice-cream. Upon the latter set some Kirsch-flavored stewed cherries, and cover the latter with raspberry *purée*.

2803—COUPES EUGENIE   *Coupes Eugenie*

Fill the bowls with vanilla ice-cream, combined with broken candied chestnuts. Cover the ice with whipped cream and upon the latter sprinkle some crystallized violets.

2804—COUPES A LA FAVORITE   *Coupes à la Favorite*

Fill the bowls vertically, half with Kirsch-Maraschino-flavored ice, and half with vanilla ice-cream. Border them with a thread of pineapple ice, and in the middle set some whipped cream combined with strawberry *purée*.

2805—COUPES GERMAINE   *Coupes Germaine*

Fill the bottom of the bowls with vanilla ice, and distribute over it half-sugared cherries, steeped in Kirsch. Cover the cherries with a dry *purée* of chestnuts, squeezed out to resemble vermicelli, and border the bowls with whipped cream.

2806—COUPES GRESSAC   *Coupes Gressac*

Fill the bottom of the bowls with vanilla ice-cream, and upon the latter in each bowl set three small macaroons, saturated with Kirsch. Upon the macaroons set an overturned *poached* half-peach, the hollow of which should be garnished with Bar red-currant jam. Surround the peaches with a border of whipped cream.

2807—COUPES JACQUES   *Coupes Jacques*

Fill the bowls vertically, half with lemon and half with strawberry ice. Between the two ices, on top of the bowl, set a tablespoon of a *macedoine* of fresh fruit, steeped in Kirsch.

2808—COUPES A LA MALMAISON   *Coupes à la Malmaison*

Fill the bowls with vanilla ice-cream, combined with peeled Muscadel grapes. Veil with spun sugar.

2809—COUPES A LA MEXICAINE   *Coupes à la Mexicaine*

Fill the bowls with tangerine ice, combined with pineapple cut into very small dice.

2810—COUPES MIREILLE   *Coupes Mireille*

Fill the bowls, half with vanilla ice-cream, and half with redcurrant ice with cream. In the middle of each bowl set a nectarine *poached* in vanilla-flavored syrup, the stone of which should be replaced by Bar white-currant jam.

Decorate with whipped cream, and cover with a veil of spun sugar.

2811—COUPES PETIT DUC   *Coupes Petit Duc*

Fill the bowls with vanilla ice-cream. Set in each a *poached* half-peach garnished with Bar red-currant jam. Surround the peaches with a ribbon of lemon ice.

2812—COUPES REVE DE BEBE   *Coupes Rêve de Bébé*

Fill the bowls, half with pineapple ice and half with raspberry ice. Between the two ices set a line of small strawberries, steeped in orange juice. Border the bowls with whipped cream, and sprinkle the latter with crystallized violets.

2813—COUPES MADAME SANS-GENE   *Coupes Madame Sans-Gêne*

Fill the bottom and sides of the bowls with a layer of vanilla ice-cream. Fill them with Bar red-currant jam, and cover the latter, by means of a spoon, with whipped cream.

2814—COUPES TUTTI-FRUTTI   *Coupes Tutti-Frutti*

Sprinkle the bottom of the bowls with various fresh fruits cut into dice; garnish the bowls with strawberry, pineapple and lemon ices, spread alternately with layers of the same fruits.

2815—COUPES VENUS   *Coupes Vénus*

Half-fill the bowls with vanilla ice-cream.

In the middle of each bowl set a small peach, *poached* in vanilla-flavored syrup, with a very red, small cherry upon it.

Border the peaches with a ribbon of whipped cream.

2816—LIGHT ICES   *Glaces Légéres*

These ices differ from those dealt with above, in that they are moulded and frozen directly, without being kept in the freezer.

To this class belong the ices most commonly served and the best; and, since their preparation requires no special utensils, they may be served everywhere: such are the "Iced Biscuits," the "Bombes," the *"Mousses,"* the *"Parfaits,"* the "Puddings," and the "Iced *Soufflés.*"

These different kinds of ices greatly resemble one another, and their names, which are puzzling at times, are only a matter of fancy.

2817—VARIOUS PREPARATIONS   *Préparations Diverses*

The old iced-biscuit preparation consisted of an English custard (2398), prepared from one lb. of sugar, twelve egg-yolks, and one pint of milk.

When the custard was cooked, it used to be strained into a bowl, left to cool (being fanned the while), and then placed upon ice, and finished with the whisk. Originally this cream was moulded at this stage; but now it is customary to add one quart of whipped cream to it; which operation makes the recipe more like that of a Bombe, which, in its turn, resembles that of the preparation for *Mousses.*

ICED BISCUITS

2818—PREPARATION FOR ICED BISCUITS
Préparation pour Biscuits Glacés

Beat in a copper basin, in a *bain-marie* (water-bath), twelve egg-yolks and one lb. of powdered sugar, until the paste gets very firm and reaches the ribbon-stage (2376).

Take the basin off the fire, and whisk until the whole is quite cold. Then, add eight oz. of Italian *meringue* (2383) and one pint of whipped cream.

2819—THE MOULDING OF ICED BISCUITS
Moulage de Biscuits Glacés

These biscuits are moulded in rectangular brick-shaped cases, fitted with lids, top and bottom.

Generally, the preparation moulded in the covers is of a different flavor and color from the one filling the middle of the mould.

For example, one of the covers may be garnished with strawberry, and the other with violet preparation, while the central portion may hold a vanilla-flavored preparation. After having frozen them for three hours, in a pail filled with freezing ice, and turned them out, these bricks are cut up vertically into rectangles, on the cut sides of which the differently colored layers are distinctly marked. Place these rectangles in special paper cases; decorate them on top, if the directions permit it, and place them in a refrigerator until about to serve.

Nearly all Bombe preparations may become the base of biscuits, which are then named after them; *e.g.:* from Bombe Odessa, Odessa Iced Biscuits may be prepared.

Various Iced Biscuits

2820—BENEDICTINE ICED BISCUIT   *Biscuit Glacé Bénédictine*
Mould the base with strawberry ice, the middle with Bénédictine ice, and the top with violet ice. Freeze and cut up as directed.

2821—MARQUISE ICED BISCUIT   *Biscuit Glacé Marquise*
Mould with Kirsch and strawberry ices, alternated twice.

2822—MONT BLANC ICED BISCUIT   *Biscuit Glacé Mont-Blanc*
Mould the base with a rum-flavored preparation, the middle with a chestnut preparation, and the top with a vanilla-flavored preparation.

2823—NEAPOLITAN ICED BISCUIT   *Biscuit Glacé Napolitaine*
Mould the base with a vanilla-flavored preparation, the middle with strawberry ice, and the top with a preparation of *pralined* biscuit.

2824—PRINCESSE ICED BISCUIT   *Biscuit Glacé Princesse*
Mould and leave to set a biscuit-*pralined* preparation. After having cut up the moulding, surround it with slivered and *pralined* almonds.

Decorate the pieces with vanilla ice-cream and tangerine ice.

2825—SIGURD ICED BISCUIT   *Biscuit Glacé Sigurd*

Mould the base with strawberry and the top with pistachio biscuit preparation. When the biscuit is frozen, cut it into rectangular slices, and sandwich each slice between two sugar wafers.

2826—BOMBES (General Recipe)   *Bombes*

Originally, Bombes were made from an ordinary ice preparation, in spherical moulds; hence their name, which is once more justified by their arrangement, consisting as it used to do of superimposed and circular layers, the outermost of which was very thin. Nowadays, Bombes are more often moulded in the shape of shells, but the preparation from which they are made is much more delicate than it was formerly.

2827—PREPARATION FOR BOMBES   *Préparation pour Bombes*

Gradually mix thirty-two egg-yolks with one quart of syrup at 28°. Put the whole on a very moderate fire, whisking it as for a *Génoise*, and, when the preparation is firm enough and taken off the fire, continue whisking it over ice until it is quite cold. Then add the selected flavor, and one and one-third quarts of stiffly-whipped cream.

2828—THE MOULDING OF BOMBES   *Moulage de Bombes*

First coat the bottom and sides of a mould with the ice preparation denoted by the name of the Bombe. This coat, which should vary in thickness in accordance with the size of the mould, should be somewhat thin, and made from an ordinary ice preparation, which is suited better than any other kind to this class of dish.

The middle is then filled with a Bombe preparation, flavored as directed, or with a *Mousse* preparation. The whole is then covered with a round piece of white paper, and the mould is hermetically sealed with its cover, set to freeze, and left for two or three hours in the ice.

When about to serve, take the mould out of the ice; wash it with cold water; dip it quickly in tepid water; dry it with a towel, and overturn the mould on a napkin or on a block of ice.

VARIOUS BOMBES

2829—BOMBE ABOUKIR   *Bombe Aboukir*

Having coated the mould with pistachio ice, fill it with a *pralined* Bombe-preparation, combined with chopped pistachios.

2830—BOMBE AFRICAINE *Bombe Africaine*

Coat the mould with chocolate ice, and fill it with an apricot Bombe-preparation.

2831—BOMBE ABRICOTINE *Bombe Abricotine*

Coat the mould with apricot ice, and fill it with a Kirsch-flavored Bombe-preparation, laid in alternate layers with stewed apricots.

2832—BOMBE AIDA *Bombe Aïda*

Coat the mould with strawberry ice, and fill it with a Kirsch-flavored Bombe-preparation.

2833—BOMBE ALMERIA *Bombe Almeria*

Coat the mould with Anisette ice, and fill it with a pomegranate Bombe-preparation.

2834—BOMBE ALHAMBRA *Bombe Alhambra*

Coat the mould with vanilla ice-cream, and garnish it with a strawberry Bombe-preparation. After turning it out surround the Bombe with a crown of fine strawberries steeped in Kirsch.

2835—BOMBE AMERICAINE *Bombe Américaine*

Coat the mould with strawberry ice, and fill it with a tangerine Bombe-preparation. After turning out decorate the Bombe with pistachio ice.

2836—BOMBE ANDALOUSE *Bombe Andalouse*

Coat the mould with apricot ice, and fill it with a vanilla Bombe-preparation.

2837—BOMBE BATAVIA *Bombe Batavia*

Coat the mould with a pineapple ice and fill it up with a strawberry Bombe-preparation, combined with candied ginger cut into dice.

2838—BOMBE BOURDALOUE *Bombe Bourdaloue*

Coat the mould with vanilla ice-cream, and fill it up with an Anisette Bombe-preparation.

After turning out decorate the Bombe with crystallized violets.

2839—BOMBE BRESILIENNE *Bombe Brésilienne*

Coat the mould with pineapple ice, and fill it with a vanilla and rum Bombe-preparation combined with pineapple dice.

2840—BOMBE CAMARGO   *Bombe Camargo*
Coat the mould with coffee ice, and fill it with a vanilla Bombe-preparation.

2841—BOMBE CARDINAL   *Bombe Cardinal*
Coat the mould with a red-currant and raspberry ice, and fill it with a *pralined* vanilla Bombe-preparation.

2842—BOMBE CEYLAN   *Bombe Ceylan*
Coat the mould with coffee ice and fill it with a rum Bombe-preparation.

2843—BOMBE CHATEAUBRIAND   *Bombe Châteaubriand*
Coat the mould with apricot ice, and fill it with a vanilla Bombe-preparation.

2844—BOMBE CLARENCE   *Bombe Clarence*
Coat the mould with banana ice, and fill it with a violet Bombe-preparation.

2845—BOMBE COLOMBIA   *Bombe Colombia*
Coat the mould with Kirsch ice, and fill it with a pear Bombe-preparation. After turning out decorate the Bombe with half-sugared cherries.

2846—BOMBE COPPELIA   *Bombe Coppélia*
Coat the mould with coffee ice and fill it with a *pralined* Bombe-preparation.

2847—BOMBE CZARINE   *Bombe Czarine*
Coat the mould with vanilla ice, and fill it with a Kümmel Bombe-preparation. After turning out decorate it with crystallized violets.

2848—BOMBE DAME-BLANCHE   *Bombe Dame-Blanche*
Coat the mould with vanilla ice, and fill it with an almond milk Bombe-preparation.

2849—BOMBE DANICHEFF   *Bombe Danicheff*
Coat the mould with coffee ice, and fill it with a Kirsch Bombe-preparation.

2850—BOMBE DIABLE ROSE   *Bombe Diable Rose*
Coat the mould with strawberry ice, and fill it with a Kirsch Bombe-preparation, combined with half-sugared cherries.

2851—BOMBE DIPLOMATE   *Bombe Diplomate*
Coat the mould with vanilla ice-cream, and fill it with a Maraschino Bombe-preparation, combined with candied fruit.

ICES

2852—BOMBE DUCHESSE   *Bombe Duchesse*
Coat the mould with banana-ice, and fill it with a pear Bombe-preparation flavored with Kirsch.

2853—BOMBE FANCHON   *Bombe Fanchon*
Coat the mould with *pralined* ice, and fill it with a Kirsch Bombe-preparation, containing some coffee-drops.

2854—BOMBE FEDORA   *Bombe Fedora*
Coat the mould with orange ice, and fill it with a *pralined* Bombe-preparation.

2855—BOMBE FLORENTINE   *Bombe Florentine*
Coat the mould with raspberry ice, and fill it with a *pralined* Bombe-preparation.

2856—BOMBE FORMOSA   *Bombe Formosa*
Coat the mould with vanilla ice-cream, and fill it with a strawberry Bombe-preparation, combined with big strawberries.

2857—BOMBE FRANCILLON   *Bombe Francillon*
Coat the mould with coffee ice, and fill it with a Bombe-preparation flavored with liqueur-brandy.

2858—BOMBE FROU-FROU   *Bombe Frou-Frou*
Coat the mould with vanilla ice-cream, and fill it with a rum Bombe-preparation, combined with candied fruit.

2859—BOMBE GRANDE DUCHESSE   *Bombe Grande Duchesse*
Coat the mould with pear ice, and fill it with a Chartreuse Bombe-preparation.

2860—BOMBE GISMONDA   *Bombe Gismonda*
Coat the mould with *pralined* ice, and fill it with an Anisette Bombe-preparation, combined with Bar white-currant jam.

2861—BOMBE HAVANAISE   *Bombe Havanaise*
Coat the mould with coffee ice, and fill it with a vanilla and rum
Bombe-preparation.

2862—BOMBE HILDA   *Bombe Hilda*
Coat the mould with filbert ice, and fill it with a Chartreuse
Bombe-preparation, combined with filbert *pralin*.

2863—BOMBE HOLLANDAISE   *Bombe Hollandaise*
Coat the mould with vanilla ice-cream, and fill it with a Curaçao
Bombe-preparation.

2864—BOMBE JAFFA   *Bombe Jaffa*
Coat the mould with *pralined* ice, and fill it with an orange
Bombe-preparation.

2865—BOMBE JAPONAISE   *Bombe Japonaise*
Coat the mould with peach ice, and fill it with a tea *mousse*-
preparation.

2866—BOMBE JEANNE D'ARC   *Bombe Jeanne D'Arc*
Coat the mould with vanilla ice-cream, and fill it with a chocolate
pralined Bombe-preparation.

2867—BOMBE JOSEPHINE   *Bombe Joséphine*
Coat the mould with coffee ice, and fill it with a pistachio Bombe-
preparation.

2868—BOMBE MADELEINE   *Bombe Madeleine*
Coat the mould with almond ice, and fill it with a vanilla and
Kirsch Bombe-preparation, combined with candied fruit.

2869—BOMBE MALTAISE   *Bombe Maltaise*
Coat the mould with blood-orange ice, and fill it with tangerine-
flavored whipped cream.

2870—BOMBE A LA MARECHALE   *Bombe a la Maréchale*
Coat the mould with strawberry ice, and fill it with alternate
layers of pistachio, orange and vanilla Bombe-preparation.

2871—BOMBE MARGOT   *Bombe Margot*
Coat the mould with almond ice, and fill it with pistachio Bombe-
preparation. After turning out, decorate with vanilla ice-cream.

2872—BOMBE MARIE LOUISE   *Bombe Marie Louise*
Coat the mould with raspberry ice, and fill it with a vanilla Bombe-preparation.

2873—BOMBE MARQUISE   *Bombe Marquise*
Coat the mould with apricot ice, and fill it with a Champagne Bombe-preparation.

2874—BOMBE MASCOTTE   *Bombe Mascotte*
Coat the mould with peach-ice, and fill it with a Kirsch Bombe-preparation.

2875—BOMBE MATHILDE   *Bombe Mathilde*
Coat the mould with coffee ice, and fill it with an apricot Bombe-preparation.

2876—BOMBE MEDICIS   *Bombe Médicis*
Coat the mould with brandy ice, and fill it with a raspberry Bombe-preparation.

2877—BOMBE MERCEDES   *Bombe Mercédês*
Coat the mould with apricot ice, and fill it with a Chartreuse Bombe-preparation.

2878—BOMBE MIGNON   *Bombe Mignon*
Coat the mould with apricot ice, and fill it with nut Bombe-preparation.

2879—BOMBE MISS HELYETT   *Bombe Miss Helyett*
Coat the mould with raspberry ice, and fill it with a vanilla Bombe-preparation.

2880—BOMBE MOGADOR   *Bombe Mogador*
Coat the mould with coffee ice, and fill it with a Kirsch Bombe-preparation.

2881—BOMBE MOLDAVE   *Bombe Moldave*
Coat the mould with pineapple ice, and fill it with a Curaçao Bombe-preparation.

2882—BOMBE MONTMORENCY   *Bombe Montmorency*
Coat the mould with Kirsch ice, and fill it with a cherry Bombe-preparation. After turning out, surround it with half-candied cherries.

2883—BOMBE MOSCOVITE   *Bombe Moscovite*

Coat the mould with Kümmel ice, and fill it with a bitter-almond Bombe-preparation, combined with candied fruit.

2884—BOMBE MOUSSELINE   *Bombe Mousseline*

Coat the mould with strawberry ice, and fill it with whipped cream, combined with strawberry *purée*.

2885—BOMBE NABAB   *Bombe Nabab*

Coat the mould with *pralined* ice, and fill it with a liqueur-brandy Bombe-preparation, containing candied fruit.

2886—BOMBE NELUSKO   *Bombe Nélusko*

Coat the mould with filbert *pralined* ice, and fill it with a chocolate Bombe-preparation.

2887—BOMBE NERO   *Bombe Nero*

Take a *dome-mould* and coat it with vanilla ice-cream with caramel; fill it with vanilla *mousse,* combined with small, imitation truffles, the size of small nuts, made from chocolate.

Turn out the Bombe on a thin cushion of Punch Biscuit (2381), of the same diameter as the Bombe. Cover the whole with a thin layer of Italian *meringue* (2383); and, on top, set a small receptacle made of Italian *meringue* dried in an almost cold oven. Decorate the sides by means of a pastry-bag with *meringue,* and set the whole in the oven to *glaze* quickly.

On taking the Bombe out of the oven, pour some hot rum into the bowl, and light it when serving.

2888—BOMBE SAINT LAUD   *Bombe Saint Laud*

Coat the mould with raspberry ice, and fill it with alternate layers of melon Bombe-preparation and whipped cream.

2889—BOMBE NESSELRODE   *Bombe Nesselrode*

Coat the mould with vanilla ice-cream, and fill it with whipped cream, combined with chestnut *purée*.

2890—BOMBE ODETTE   *Bombe Odette*

Coat the mould with vanilla ice-cream, and fill it with a *pralined* Bombe-preparation.

2891—BOMBE ODESSA   *Bombe Odessa*

Coat the mould with apricot ice, and fill it with a strawberry Bombe-preparation.

2892—BOMBE ORIENTALE　　　　　*Bombe Orientale*
Coat the mould with ginger ice, and fill it with a pistachio Bombe-preparation.

2893—BOMBE PATRICIENNE　　　　*Bombe Patricienne*
Coat the mould with vanilla ice-cream, and fill it with a *pralin* and chocolate Bombe-preparation.

2894—BOMBE PETIT DUC　　　　　*Bombe Petit Duc*
Coat the mould with strawberry ice, and fill it with a hazel-nut Bombe-preparation, combined with Bar red-currant jam.

2895—BOMBE POMPADOUR　　　　*Bombe Pompadour*
Coat the mould with asparagus ice, and fill it with a pomegranate Bombe-preparation.

2896—BOMBE PROPHETE　　　　　*Bombe Prophête*
Coat the mould with strawberry ice, and fill it with pineapple preparation.

2897—BOMBE RICHELIEU　　　　　*Bombe Richelieu*
Coat the mould with rum ice; fill it with a coffee Bombe-preparation, and distribute coffee drops upon it after turning.

2898—BOMBE ROSETTE　　　　　*Bombe Rosette*
Coat the mould with vanilla ice-cream, and fill it up with red-currant-flavored whipped cream, combined with red-currants.

2899—BOMBE A LA ROYALE　　　　*Bombe a La Royale*
Coat the mould with Kirsch ice, and fill it with a chocolate *pralined* Bombe-preparation.

2900—BOMBE SANTIAGO　　　　　*Bombe Santiago*
Coat the mould with Brandy ice, and fill it with a pistachio Bombe-preparation.

2901—BOMBE SELIKA　　　　　*Bombe Sélika*
Coat the mould with *pralined* ice, and fill it with a Curaçao Bombe-preparation.

2902—BOMBE SKOBELEFF　　　　*Bombe Skobeleff*
Coat the mould with Vodka ice, and fill it with Kümmel-flavored whipped cream.

2903—BOMBE STROGOFF   *Bombe Strogoff*
Coat the mould with peach ice, and fill it with a Champagne
Bombe-preparation.

2904—BOMBE SUCCES   *Bombe Succès*
Coat the mould with apricot ice, and fill it with Kirsch-flavored
whipped cream, combined with candied apricots cut into dice.

2905—BOMBE SULTANE   *Bombe Sultane*
Coat the mould with chocolate ice, and fill it with a *pralined*
Bombe-preparation.

2906—BOMBE SUZANNE   *Bombe Suzanne*
Coat the mould with pink rum ice, and fill it with vanilla Bombe-
preparation, combined with Bar red-currant jam.

2907—BOMBE TORTONI   *Bombe Tortoni*
Coat the mould with *pralined* ice, and fill it with coffee Bombe-
preparation, containing coffee beans.

2908—BOMBE TOSCA   *Bombe Tosca*
Coat the mould with apricot ice, and fill it with a Maraschino
and fruit Bombe-preparation. After turning out, decorate the Bombe
with lemon ice.

2909—BOMBE TROCADERO   *Bombe Trocadéro*
Coat the mould with orange ice, combined with candied orange-
rind, cut into small dice; and fill with alternate layers of whipped
cream and slices of filbert *Génoise,* cut in graduated sizes, and saturated with Curaçao syrup. Sprinkle some orange-*zest* dice on each
slice of *Génoise.*

2910—BOMBE TUTTI-FRUTTI   *Bombe Tutti-Frutti*
Coat the mould with strawberry ice, and fill it with a lemon
Bombe-preparation, combined with various candied fruits, cut into
dice.

2911—BOMBE A LA VALENCAY   *Bombe a la Valençay*
Coat the mould with *pralined* ice, and fill it with whipped cream,
combined with raspberries.

2912—BOMBE VENITIENNE   *Bombe Vénitienne*
Coat the mould half with vanilla and half with strawberry ice
and fill it with a Maraschino and Kirsch Bombe-preparation.

2913—BOMBE VICTORIA   *Bombe Victoria*
Coat the mould with strawberry ice, and fill it with Plombière ice.

2914—BOMBE ZAMORA   *Bombe Zamora*
Coat the mould with coffee ice, and fill it with a Curaçao Bombe-
preparation.

Iced Mousses

The composition for *mousses* is prepared either from English
cream (2397) or from syrup. The last method is specially suited to
fruit *mousses*.

2915—PREPARATION FOR ICED FRUIT MOUSSES
Composition de Mousse Glacée aux Fruits
This is a cold syrup at 35°, to which is added an equal quantity
of a *purée* of the fruit under treatment, and twice that amount of
very stiff whipped cream.

2916—PREPARATION OF ICED MOUSSE WITH CREAM
Composition de Mousse Glacée à la Crème
Make an English cream from one lb. of powdered sugar, sixteen
egg-yolks, and one pint of milk, and leave it to cool.
When it is quite cold, add to it one pint of raw cream, two-thirds
oz. of powdered tragacanth gum, and the flavor which is to characterize the preparation.
If the *mousse* be a fruit one, add to it one pint of a *purée* of fresh
fruit.
Beat over ice, until the preparation gets very frothy; put it into
moulds, lined with white paper; thoroughly close them, and keep
them in a refrigerator for two or three hours, subject to their size.

2917—VARIOUS ICED MOUSSES   *Mousses Glacées Diverses*
After the same procedure, *mousses* may be prepared with Anisette,
Coffee, Chocolate, Kirsch, Maraschino, Rum, Tea, etc.; Apricots,
Strawberries, Oranges and Tangerines, fresh Walnuts, Peaches,
Vanilla, Violets, etc.

2918—PARFAIT (General Recipe)   *Parfait*

Mix thirty egg-yolks with one quart of cold syrup at 28°. Put the mixture on a slow fire, and cook it as for an English cream; strain it and whisk it over ice until it is quite cold.

Add three pints of very stiff, whipped cream and one-fifth pint of brandy or rum, in order to finish it; mould the preparation in *Parfait moulds*, and pack them in a freezer for from two to three hours.

N.B.—The term *"Parfait,"* which, formerly, was applied only to *"Parfait au Café,"* has become the common name for uncoated ices, made from Bombe-preparations having but one flavor. And this is fairly logical, seeing that Bombe-preparations, but for a few insignificant distinctions, are exactly like *Parfait*-preparation.

It is therefore just as reasonable to make vanilla, chocolate, and *pralined Parfaits*, etc., as to make them with coffee.

2919—ICED PUDDINGS   *Puddings Glacés*

Preparations of this class follow no hard and fast rules, and, in reality, they are not ices at all. They are nothing else than iced desserts, the bases of which generally consist of thick English custard, the same as that which serves in the preparation of Bavarois.

The few following recipes, however, are exceptions to this rule.

2920—PUDDING DE CASTRIES   *Pudding de Castries*

Coat a Bombe mould with a thin layer of vanilla ice-cream, and fill it with two Bombe-preparations, spread in somewhat thick, alternate layers. One of the preparations should be of vanilla, on each thickness of which a layer of lady fingers, cut into dice and sprinkled with Anisette, should be spread; and the other preparation should be of tangerine.

Between the layers, sprinkle a few pinches of grated chocolate, and fill up the mould with a thickness of vanilla ice-cream.

Thoroughly close the utensil; pack it for about two or three hours. Turn it out on a folded napkin; sprinkle on a few red, crushed *pralins;* and serve an iced tangerine syrup separately.

2921—MARIE-ROSE PUDDING   *Pudding Marie-Rose*

Line a *Charlotte-mould* with rolled *gaufrettes* (thin wafers); placing them snugly one against the other. By means of a pastry-bag, fill the *gaufrettes* with very stiff strawberry ice, and then fill the mould with a vanilla *pralined* Bombe-preparation. Keep the mould in the refrigerator for three hours, and turn out the pudding on a napkin. Decorate it on top with pink and white whipped cream. Serve a chocolate ice-cream separately.

2922—MIRAMAR PUDDING   *Pudding Miramar*

Fill an iced *Madeleine-mould* with lady fingers, saturated with Chartreuse, and alternate them with thin slices of fresh pineapple, saturated in Kirsch, and pipped sections of tangerine, skinned.

Fill up the mould with a Bombe-preparation of pomegranate juice, flavored with Kirsch; close the mould, keep it in ice for two hours, and turn out the pudding on a napkin when about to serve.

Serve an iced vanilla syrup separately.

2923—SEYMOUR PUDDING   *Pudding Seymour*

Cut a *Mousseline* Brioche into thin slices, and set these to soak in raw, sweetened and Kirsch-flavored cream. Peel and finely slice some peaches, and *poach* them in vanilla-flavored syrup; also peel some very ripe Bartlett pears.

Prepare a pink Bombe-preparation, flavored with Kirsch and *Orgeat;* and then fill up the mould with alternate layers of the slices of brioche and fruit, with Bar red-currant jam added; and the Bombe-preparation.

Close the mould, keep it in ice for two hours, and turn out the pudding on a napkin.

2924—ICED SOUFFLES   *Soufflés Glacés*

The preparation differs according as to whether the *Soufflés* be prepared with fruit, or with such flavors as vanilla, coffee, chocolate, etc.

The last named are made with the Iced-*Mousse* preparation (2916), which may also serve for the fruit *Soufflés*, but, in the case of the latter, the following preparation is preferable:—

Whip the whites of ten eggs to a very stiff froth, and add to this one and one-tenth lbs. of sugar cooked to the *small-crack* (285° F.) stage. Transfer the whole to a bowl; flavor according to fancy, and add one pint of a *purée* of fruit and one pint of very stiffly-whipped cream.

2925—THE MOULDING OF LARGE AND SMALL ICED SOUFFLES
Moulage des Gros et des Petits Soufflés Glacés

Mould the large ones in ordinary *Soufflé timbales,* which should be lined with bands of white paper, fixed with butter, and over-reaching the edges of the *timbales* by one and a half to two inches, that the preparation, in projecting above the brims of the utensils, may appear like a *Soufflé* when the paper is removed.

The small *Soufflés* are moulded in cases or in small silver *cassolettes,* which are likewise wrapped in bands of paper, that the preparation may rise above their brims. As soon as they are moulded, put the *Soufflés* in a very cold refrigerator; and when about to serve them, carefully remove the bands of paper which, once the preparation has solidified, have served their purpose; and serve the cases or silver *cassolettes* on a napkin or on a carved block of ice.

Like the Bombes, and the Iced Biscuits, Iced *Soufflés* may be indefinitely varied, owing to the many combinations to which they lend themselves.

2926—SHERBETS *Sorbets*

Sherbets and their derivative preparations consist of very light and barely-congealed ices, served after the Entrées. They serve in freshening the stomach; preparing it to properly receive the roast.

They are appetizers and help to aid digestion.

2927—PREPARATION FOR SHERBETS *Préparation pour Sorbets*

Sherbets are made from any liqueur ice preparation at 15°; or they may be prepared as follows:—For one quart of preparation, take the juice of two lemons and one orange, half-a-pint of port wine, of Samos wine, of Sauterne, or other good wine; and add cold syrup at 22°, until the saccharometer registers 15°.

For liqueur sherbets, allow about one-fifth pint of liqueur per quart of the preparation; but remember that this is subject to the kind of liqueur used. For the quantity just prescribed, use syrup at 18° or 19°, which the subsequent addition of liqueur reduces to the proper degree. Whatever be the kind of liqueur, the latter should only be added when the Sherbet is completely frozen; that is to say, at the last moment.

Fruit sherbets are generally prepared from the juices and syrups of juicy fruits. Fruit *purées* are scarcely suited to this mode of procedure, and they are only resorted to in exceptional cases.

The Freezing of Sherbets.—Pour the preparation into the freezer, which should have been previously packed, and keep the utensil moving. Remove portions of the preparation from the sides of the receptacle as fast as they adhere, and mix them with the whole. until the latter is completely congealed; remembering not to stir at all during the freezing process. When the preparation is firm enough, mix with it, gently, the quarter of its weight of Italian *meringue* (2383) or very stiffly whipped cream; and finish by the addition of the liqueur.

The Serving of Sherbets.—Take some of the Sherbet preparation in a spoon, and set it in Sherbet or Sherry glasses, shaping it to a point.

When the Sherbet is prepared with wine, sprinkle the preparation when it is in the glasses with a tablespoon of the selected wine.

The consistency of a Sherbet, of any kind, should be such as to permit it being drunk.

2928—VARIOUS SHERBETS   *Sorbets Divers*

Having pointed out that Sherbets may be prepared from the juices of every fruit such as pineapple, cherries, strawberries, raspberries, red-currants, etc., and from every wine and liqueur such as Port, Samos wine, Marsala, Johannisburg, Rum, Kirsch, Liqueur-Brandy, etc., and since the procedure is the same in every case, there is no need to devote a special article to each.

2929—SICILIENNE SHERBERT   *Sorbet à la Sicilienne*

Keep a very green watermelon in the refrigerator for three hours.

One hour before serving, open it on top, as directed under "Surprise Melon" (2730), and take out the seeds.

Then, loosen the pulp with a silver spoon, without taking it from the fruit; sprinkle it with Maraschino, and put the whole back into the refrigerator.

Serve on cracked ice or on a block of it, and serve the pulp before the diners in Sherbet glasses.

2930—GRANITES   *Granités*

Granités answer the same purpose as Sherbets, while they may also be introduced into certain culinary preparations.

The bases of these preparations consist of very thin syrups made from fruit juices, and not overreaching fourteen degrees (saccharometer).

Granités consist only of iced syrups, and are not combined with any Italian or other *meringue*.

As in the case of the Sherbets, but more particularly in regard to these, the cook should remember not to stir the syrup during the freezing process, lest it separate; and, when it is congealed, it should form a light, granulated mass.

2931—MARQUISES   *Marquises*

Marquises are generally made from strawberries or pineapple, with Kirsch. The preparation is that of a Sherbet with Kirsch, registering 17° by the saccharometer. The freezing is the same as for *Granités;* but it should be carried a little further.

When about to serve, mix the preparation per pint with half a pint of very stiff whipped cream, combined with a strawberry or pineapple *purée,* subject to the purpose of the Marquise.

2932—ROMAINE PUNCH   *Punch à la Romaine*

Mix sufficient amount dry white wine, or dry champagne, with one pint of syrup at 22°, to reduce the latter to 17°; add the juice of two oranges and two lemons, a strip of orange and lemon *zest,* and let infusion proceed for one hour.

Strain the syrup and bring it to 18°.

Freeze until it is somewhat stiff, and mix it with the quarter of its volume of Italian *meringue* (2383) (prepared from two egg-whites and three and a half oz. of sugar).

When about to serve, complete with one-fifth pint of Rum, added little by little.

Serve the preparation in glasses, after the style of the Sherbets.

N.B.—For all Sherbets and Punches, one quart of the finished preparation should be allowed for every ten people.

2933—SPOOMS   *Spooms*

Spoom is a kind of Sherbet prepared from a syrup at 20°. Add to it twice as much Italian *meringue* (2383) as was added to the Sherbets. Do not work it too briskly, that it may remain very light and frothy.

Spooms are made from fruit juices; but more often from such wines as Champagne, Samos, Muscat, Zucco, etc.

Serve it in glasses like the Sherbets.

APPENDIX

(Following are the recipes referred to in the main body of the book. The identifying numbers are those originally given to the recipes in the complete American edition of THE ESCOFFIER COOK BOOK.)

174—ANGLAISE (FOR EGG-AND-BREAD-CRUMBLING)

Panés à l'Anglaise

It is well to have this always ready for those dishes which are to be *panés à l'anglaise* (breaded), or as many of the recipes direct: *treated à l'anglaise.*

It is made of well-beaten eggs, salt, pepper and one teaspoon of oil per egg.

Its Uses.—The solids to be *panés à l'anglaise* (breaded) are dipped into the preparation described above taking care that the latter coats them thoroughly; whereupon, according to the requirements, they are rolled either in bread-crumbs or in fine *raspings*. From this combination of egg with bread-crumbs or *raspings* there results a kind of coat which, at the moment of contact with the hot fat, is immediately converted into a resisting crust. In croquettes this crust checks the escape, into the fat, of the substances it encloses, and this is more especially the case when the croquettes contain some reduced sauce, or are composed of uncooked meats or fish whose juices are thereby entirely retained. A solid food prepared *à l'anglaise* and cooked in fat should always be put into the fat when this is very hot, so as to ensure the instantaneous solidification of the egg and bread-crumbs.

N.B.—Foods to be treated *à l'anglaise* are generally rolled in flour before being immersed in the *anglaise*, for the flour helps the bread-crumbs and egg to adhere to the food.

The crust formed over the food thus acquires a density which is indispensable.

175—CLARIFIED BUTTER

Beurre Clarifié

A certain quantity of clarified butter should always be kept ready and handy.

To prepare this butter, put one lb. to melt in a saucepan large enough to hold twice that amount. Place the saucepan on the fire, over moderate heat; remove all the scum which rises to the surface, and, when the butter looks quite clear and all foreign substances have dropped to the bottom, strain it through muslin and put the liquid carefully away.

141

234—BATTER FOR OVEN-GLAZED FRUIT FRITTERS

Pâté à Frire pour Beignets Glacés au Four

Mix one lb. of flour with two tablespoons of oil, a few grains of salt, two eggs (added one after the other), the necessary quantity of water, and one oz. of sugar. Keep this preparation in a lukewarm place to let it ferment, and stir it with a wooden spoon before using it to cover the food.

Remarks.—Batter for fruit fritters may contain a few tablespoons of brandy, in which case an equal quantity of the water must be eliminated.

249—POACHINGS   *Les Pochés*

However nonsensical it may sound, the best possible definition of a *poaching* is a boiling that does not boil. The term *poach* is extended to all slow processes of cooking which involve the use of a liquor, however small. Thus the term *poach* applies to the cooking in *court-bouillon* of large pieces of turbot and salmon, as well as to fillets of sole cooked with a little fish *fumet,* to hot *mousselines* and *mousses,* cooked in moulds, to *quenelles* which are cooked in salted water, to eggs announced as *"poached,"* to creams, various *royales,* etc. It will readily be seen that among so many different products, the time allowed for the cooking in each case must differ sometimes widely from the rest. The treatment of them all, however, is subject to this unalterable principle, namely, that the *poaching* liquor must not boil, though it should reach a degree of heat as approximate as possible to the boiling-point. Another principle is that large pieces of fish or poultry be set to boil in cold liquor, after which the latter is brought to the required temperature as rapidly as possible. The case may be the same with fillets of sole, or poultry, which are *poached* almost dry; but all other preparations whose mode of cooking is *poaching* gain by being immersed in liquor which has reached the required temperature beforehand.

Having regard to the many forms and kinds of products that are *poached,* it would be somewhat difficult to state here the details and peculiarities proper to each in the matter of *poaching;* I think, therefore, I should do better to leave these details to the respective recipes of each product, though it will now be necessary to disclose the way of *poaching* poultry, if only with a view to thoroughly acquainting the reader with the theory propounded above.

Properly prepare the piece of poultry to be *poached,* and truss it with its legs folded back alongside of the breast.

If it is to be stuffed, this should be done before trussing.

If it is to be *larded* or *studded,* either with truffles, ham, or tongue, rub it when trussed on the breasts and legs with half a lemon, and dip the same portions of its body (namely, those to be *larded* or *studded*) for a few moments in boiling white stock (10). The object of this operation is to slightly stiffen the skin, thus facilitating the *larding* or *studding.*

The Cooking of the Piece of Poultry.—Having stuffed, *larded,* or *studded* it, if necessary, and having, in any case, trussed it, place it in a receptacle just large enough to hold it, and moisten with some excellent white stock previously prepared.

Set to boil, skim, put the lid on, and continue the cooking at a low simmer. It is useless to work too quickly, as the cooking would not be shortened a second by so doing. The only results would be:—

1. Too violent evaporation, which would reduce the liquor and disturb its transparency.

2. The running of a considerable risk of bursting the piece of poultry, especially when the latter is stuffed.

The fowl, or whatever it may be, is known to be cooked when, after pricking the thick of the leg close to the "drumstick," the oozing liquid is white.

Remarks.—(*a*) The need of *poaching* poultry in a receptacle just large enough to hold the bird is accounted for as follows: (1) The piece must be wholly immersed in the stock during the cooking process. (2) As the liquor used is afterwards served as an accompanying sauce to the dish, the less there is of it the more saturated does it become with the juices of the meat, and, consequently, the better it is.

(*b*) (1) The white stock used in *poaching* should be prepared beforehand, and be very clear.

(2) If the poultry were set to cook with the products constituting the stock, even if these were more than liberally apportioned, the result would be bad, for inasmuch as a fowl, for example, can only take one and one-half hours, at the most, to cook, and the time required for extracting the nutritious and flavoring principles from the ingredients of the stock would be at least six hours, it follows that the fowl would be cooking in little more than hot water, and the resulting sauce would be quite devoid of savor.

492—THE PREPARATION OF OMELETS

La Préparation des Omelettes

Heat the butter in the omelet-pan, until it gives off the characteristic nutty smell. This will not only lend an exquisite taste to the omelet, but the degree of heat reached in order to produce the aroma will be found to ensure the perfect setting of the eggs.

Pour in the beaten and seasoned eggs, and stir briskly with a fork, in order to heat the whole mass evenly. If the omelet is to be filled inside, this ought to be done now, and then the omelet should be speedily rolled up and transferred to a dish, to be finished in accordance with the taste of the diner.

When the omelet is on the dish, a piece of butter may be quickly drawn across its surface, to make it glossy.

2291—NOODLES *Nouilles*

These are generally bought ready-made. If one wishes to prepare them, the ingredients of the paste are:—one lb. of flour, one-half oz. of salt, three whole eggs, and five egg-yolks. Moisten as for an ordinary paste, roll it out twice on a board, and leave it to stand for one or two hours before cutting it up.

All macaroni recipes may be applied to noodles.

For "Nouilles à l'Alsacienne," it is usual, when the preparation is ready in the *timbale,* to sprinkle over it a few raw pieces of noodles *sautéd* in butter to a golden brown and kept very crisp.

INDEX